- To Delia Molinski
Here's to an

EXTRAORDINARY IT
GUARANTEES!

A New Way to Build Quality Throughout Your Company & Ensure Satisfaction for Your Customers

Christopher W. L. Hart

Looking forward to working together.

Chris Hart

amacom

American Management Association

New York • Atlanta • Boston • Chicago • Kansas City • San Francisco • Washington, D.C.
Brussels • Toronto • Mexico City

Library of Congress Cataloging-in-Publication Data

Hart, Christopher W. L.
    Extraordinary guarantees : a new way to build quality throughout
your company & ensure satisfaction for your customers / Christopher
W. L. Hart.
      p.   cm.
    Includes bibliographical references and index.
    ISBN 0-8144-5064-4
    1. Quality of products—United States.   2. Warranty—United
States.   3. Consumer protection—United States.   4. Consumer
satisfaction—United States.   I. Title.
    HF5415.157.H37   1993
    658.5'62—dc20   93-9252
                                                                        CIP

Printing number

10   9   8   7   6   5   4   3   2   1

Contents

Acknowledgments

Many people deserve recognition for helping me develop, test, and refine the guarantee concept or for helping me prepare this manuscript for publication, or for both.

Foremost on my list is Joan Livingston, business writer and TQM Group affiliate, who first peaked my interest in the concept of the guarantee in 1987. Intrigued by a company with the improbable name of Bugs Burger Bug Killers—whose then-peerless guarantee is cited throughout this book—she is the person who first drew my attention to BBBK and to the incredible impact an ironclad guarantee could have on organizational performance. Together we came to recognize how powerful a tool the guarantee could be in boosting quality, the area in which most of my academic work and consulting was concentrated. Joan played a pivotal role in my thinking and writing about this concept over several years.

Subsequent to learning about Bugs Burger Bug Killers, I met Al Burger and his wife, Sandee, who graciously spoke to my students at the Harvard Business School and who made the guarantee concept come alive in the classroom. I have remained friends with Al and Sandee to this day. I also want to thank Phil Bressler, a Domino's franchisee, who, like Al, used the guarantee concept as the core value in creating an organization that stood head-and-shoulders above its competition.

I also want to express my gratitude to Dan Maher, friend and affiliate, whose name, in many respects, truly belongs beside mine on the cover of this book, given his long and intensive work with me on guarantees. Our affiliation began back during my days at Harvard Business School, when I first began to recognize the revolutionary potential of the guarantee concept. Dan's help in researching existing guarantees and their pros and cons, and in brainstorming with me about what an ideal ("extraordinary") guarantee could—and should—do, provided the foundation of the fully fleshed-out concepts and prescriptive advice in the pages that follow.

In addition, during the formation of The TQM Group, Dan served as our primary in-house guarantee expert, working extensively both as a teacher introducing companies to the concept and as a consultant who helped clients actually design and implement guarantees. His contributions have been many, and this book owes its existence in large part to those contributions.

Others who gave selflessly of their time and insights during my first explorations into service guarantees were my then-colleagues at Harvard, W. Earl Sasser, Jr., and Jim Heskett. Earl has long been a friend and mentor and, as all who know him can attest, is an alarmingly quick study. When I first briefly outlined my thoughts on guarantees, his almost instantaneous response was, "Push this concept! You've hit on something truly important here." Like Jim, he helped Dan and me (indeed, pushed us) to keep working at the concept and refining it until we fully understood not only how to convey the essential elements of the guarantee to others but also how to provide practical, action-oriented advice to managers on tapping the many benefits of the guarantee. Jim also helped me grapple with the application of the guarantee concept and provided invaluable assistance in helping me convey its power through seminars and lectures. To both of them, my deepest thanks for their contributions to my work—not just on guarantees but on quality and productivity improvement generally.

My first effort to explain the value of guarantees in writing was my 1988 *Harvard Business Review* article, "The Power of Unconditional Service Guarantees." Then-editor Ted Levitt, internationally known for his business writing and breakthrough thinking, was gracious enough in enthusiastically accepting that piece for publication to tell me, "This article will be your 'Marketing Myopia.' " If my article (and this book) ultimately has even a fraction of the impact that Ted Levitt's classic piece has had on the world of business, I will consider myself successful. And, indeed, I was gratified when my article won recognition through a *Harvard Business Review* McKinsey Award and exceptional reprint sales.

At The TQM Group, where most of my associates have worked extensively on guarantees, I would like to give particular thanks to Dan O'Brien, Steve Kett, Jim Garrett, Rishabh Mehrotra, Christina Mullin, and Bill Fleming, all of whom helped me translate the guarantee concept into a clear design-and-implementation framework that organizations can adapt to their own situations and use easily.

Kudos, next, to the many far-sighted, pioneering executives who early on recognized the significance of the guarantee concept and essentially acted as guinea pigs in implementing guarantees while I was still fine-tuning the concept. In many cases, they taught me as much about guarantees as I was able to teach them. (Given the long roster of companies we have now worked with in implementing guarantees, I will unfortunately but necessarily omit the names of some executives and managers who deserve recognition here. Suffice it to say that I, and The TQM Group, owe thanks to *every* company that has believed in the idea and worked with us to maximize its effectiveness in their own organizations.)

Among these people is a truly leading-edge thinker, Robert Gregory at First Image, the first company I worked with in guarantee design and execution. Ray Schultz and Mark Wells at Hampton Inn pushed the guarantee concept further by implementing it in a situation many would have considered untenable: a multi-site franchise organization. Similarly, Thomas Raffio of Delta Dental Plan of Massachusetts, a managed-care dental-insurance company, was an early adopter in perceiving the dramatic gains a health-services firm could reap from guarantees.

Mike Rose, CEO of what was then Holiday Corp., not only recognized the power of the guarantee but actually renamed the firm Promus—pronounced "promise"—as an explicit expression of the company's commitment to stakeholders implicit in a guarantee.

Finally, Charlie Moritz, CEO of Dun & Bradstreet, championed the guarantee concept throughout the company when it was still only a "good idea"—not the fully realized and researched concept discussed in this book.

In regard to the actual preparation of the book manuscript, thanks are due to Gary Spizizen, The TQM Group's publications director, for coordinating production; to Mike Finley, who helped me flesh out my first working draft; to Dave Freedman, whose skillful editing added clarity and organization to a long, complex manuscript; and to Mary Ellen Costello, for final proofreading.

I also want to thank Adrienne Hickey, Senior Acquisitions & Planning Editor at AMACOM Books, who saw the potential of the guarantee concept and who helped me through numerous revisions. Thanks also to Elizabeth Backman, my literary agent who introduced me to Adrienne.

I thank all these people and many more, who must go unnamed for reasons of space, for helping to make this book a reality. I hope it will help readers galvanize their organizations and achieve dramatic improvements of the sort we have witnessed in the organizations we have worked with, and I welcome and invite your comments about your experiences with guarantees, for possible later editions of this book.

Chapter 1

The Organizational Vacuum

American businesses today are plagued by a raft of problems, including low-quality products and services, low customer satisfaction, rising costs, and a loss of business to overseas competitors. The decline of the U.S. auto industry in the 1980s turned out to be a harbinger of these difficulties, which now seem to haunt all U.S. industries to some extent, from computers to banking. Japan's businesses, by contrast, are continually held up as role models of efficiency and customer satisfaction. The pervasiveness of Japanese competition is such that it is even proving a threat in the luxury hotel market in some U.S. cities, where one would think the advantage of being on home turf would be decisive.

What ails our companies? Many things, according to executives and academics, including:

■ *An inability to identify and keep track of customer needs and wants.* American businesses seem bent on turning out large quantities of products that relatively few customers want. Customers are becoming increasingly sophisticated, demanding, nonhomogeneous, and fickle, and their tastes and values are evolving at an increasingly rapid rate. U.S. companies seem always to be caught by surprise by these changes, and are often unable to address the hundreds of niches that are constantly springing up. Apparently U.S. companies haven't established the mechanisms for nailing down and addressing customer demands, and seem to lack the motivation or know-how for putting these mechanisms into place.

- *A lack of enthusiasm and commitment on the part of employees.* U.S. managers often claim their companies are at a disadvantage relative to their Japanese competitors because the U.S. work force does not share the willingness of Japanese employees to work long, hard hours or to put the needs of the company before their own personal interests. As a generalization, too many American workers do not find the workplace to be a stimulating, challenging environment. This shortage of enthusiasm and pride has a particularly negative impact in service companies, in which employee attitude is often a crucial element of the service delivery process.

- *Cumbersome, outdated organizational structures.* U.S. companies tend to be hierarchically oriented and "stovepiped" by function, department, or division. As a result, thinking usually moves in one direction only: from the top down. Even though frontline employees are closest to the customer and are in many countries regarded as a dependable source of information and ideas, most U.S. companies provide little opportunity for thinking to bubble up through the organization. Equally troubling are the barriers to horizontal information flow and task sharing in organizations; marketing, design, and manufacturing departments often cooperate awkwardly, if at all, and organizational fiefdoms resist efforts to bring down barriers.

The Fashionable Solutions

What can be done? The commonly prescribed solutions include downsizing, quality programs, and radically new organizational structures. Downsizing, which has been under way for several years in U.S. corporations, was supposed to reduce costs by removing unnecessary layers of management and excess capacity. Although the efforts have indeed cut some fat, they seem to have had only a modest impact on productivity and profitability. More discouraging, downsizing has also cut some muscle, too, in that many managers are now overloaded and crucial investment in research and development has been pared. Apparently, the problem is not that there are too many people in the company, but rather that people are not going about their jobs in the most effective ways.

The large-scale embracing of quality programs has been an attempt to examine and revamp all those systems and processes that affect the quality of products and services delivered. While this is unarguably a worthwhile goal, many companies report little improvement despite having made large investments in quality programs. Among the reasons cited for the disappointments are a lack of employee enthusiasm for the programs, the unwillingness of management to make a long-term commitment to quality and wait patiently for results, and the frustration caused by setting overly difficult goals such as zero-defect operations.

Many experts suggest that nothing short of radical organizational restructuring will fix U.S. companies. Improving the corporation, this thinking goes, requires redefining the corporation. The new corporations, as they are envisioned, will consist not of departments but of work groups, and not of management hierarchies but of networks and teams. Although there is little to argue against the superiority of these new organizational structures in dealing with the growing complexity of today's business environment, the problem is that few companies have figured out how to make the transition to the corporation of tomorrow. Instead, companies from General Motors and IBM down to the smallest businesses have found that the harder they push against existing structures, the harder the structure pushes back.

The Guarantee Edge

There is an alternative to the conventional solutions: the extraordinary guarantee. What makes a guarantee extraordinary? An ordinary guarantee (or warranty—I use the words interchangeably) is designed to alleviate the customer's loss in the case of a product or service failure—within certain limits. An extraordinary guarantee is more ambitious: In its strongest form, it promises exceptional, uncompromising quality and customer satisfaction, and backs that promise with a payout intended to fully recapture the customer's goodwill, with few strings attached.

But an extraordinary guarantee is more than a bulked-up twelve-month warranty. More important, it signals a fundamentally different way of looking at a guarantee. Where the main function of an ordinary guarantee is to reduce the customer's sense of risk at the time of purchase, an extraordinary guarantee is intended to force a company to deliver excellence and to fight to win and retain customer loyalty.

By translating every element of customer dissatisfaction into pain for the company, an extraordinary guarantee cuts through bureaucracy, breaks down barriers, creates a sense of shared mission, and sharply refocuses corporate priorities on those elements that most need fixing. By raising the bar on performance and providing a daunting but achievable goal, it energizes managers and employees and creates enthusiasm. By supplying a feedback link between customer satisfaction and operations, it not only permits a company to identify what it is that customers want and need, but, if the organization is slow to pick up on the clues, the guarantee forces the company to sit up and take notice. A company operating under an extraordinary guarantee simply can't help but do whatever it takes to get things right.

These are tall claims to make for a guarantee. But, as we shall see, there is plenty of evidence to back up these assertions. That's not to say that an extraordinary guarantee is a simple solution. In fact, designing the right extraordinary guarantee and properly implementing it can be an enormous challenge in itself—not as big a challenge as completely restructuring the corporation, but so challenging that a large percentage of the companies that try offering extraordinary guarantees end up revoking them in less than six months.

This book will help companies to avoid such mistakes by describing the various routes that can be taken to a successful extraordinary guarantee policy. First, though, we'll take a look at the evolution of the guarantee and its role in businesses. This will provide a conceptual platform from which the extraordinary guarantee can be launched.

Chapter 2

The History of Guarantees

In the middle of the nineteenth century, guarantees suddenly became important. In 1855, Cyrus McCormick began to provide a written money-back guarantee with his mechanical reapers; within a few years, John Wanamaker was offering to guarantee customer satisfaction on every item sold in his department stores. Although these two highly publicized guarantees were at first derided by most observers as financial folly, they quickly served to win over tens of thousands of customers. Before long, McCormick and Wanamaker were among the richest people in the United States. These offers not only marked the first time that guarantees were employed as a key business strategy; they also introduced the public to the notion that a guarantee could be more than a means for undoing a faulty commercial transaction. Instead, a guarantee could be a powerful statement about the way a company did business.

The Wanamaker and McCormick money-back policies represented the beginning of the transformation of the guarantee from a begrudging obligation to a powerful marketing tool. Today, a second transformation is under way. Led in large part by service companies—which, traditionally, have never offered formal guarantees—businesses are beginning to view guarantees not just as marketing tools but as a means of defining, cultivating, and maintaining quality throughout an organization. It is this second, ongoing transformation that will ultimately prove the more important of the two.

Guarantees Through the Ages

To appreciate the nature and significance of this new shift, it helps to understand the origins of guarantees. Before the

5

Wanamaker and McCormick policies, explicit guarantees were rare. Buyers relied either on their personal influence with the seller or on the legal system to obtain satisfaction on substandard purchases. Their legal rights, which were often murky, traced back to the *lex mercantoria*, or merchant law, the evolving, patchwork quilt of common law governing the sale of goods.

This unevenly interpreted and enforced body of law evolved over thousands of years of trading by the Phoenicians, Greeks, Romans, Arabs, and finally the traders of the medieval world. The laws were established by the merchants themselves at bazaars and trading fairs, where merchant-run "courts" served as arbiters of disputes. In the fourteenth century, Thomas Aquinas codified much of this informal law into a list of three assumptions, or expectations, that he held to be implicit in any sale.

1. If a purchased item has a flaw that would have been obvious to the customer at the time of purchase, and the customer buys it anyway, he cannot demand restitution from the seller.
2. If a purchased item has a less obvious defect not known to either the buyer or seller at the time of purchase, the seller must refund the buyer's money or replace the item on demand from the buyer.
3. If a purchased item has a hidden defect known to the seller, but not pointed out to the buyer, at the time of purchase, the seller must make good the purchase and expect punishment besides, having tried to perpetrate a type of fraud.[1]

The spirit of these laws is essentially that of caveat venditor, or "let the seller beware": Unless the buyer specifically knows of a problem before the time of purchase, the seller is required to provide a remedy. Also known as "implied merchantability," this view was generally enforced by such haphazard courts as could be found in the fourteenth through the fifteenth centuries.

By the beginning of the sixteenth century, however, the

burden of buyer dissatisfaction had begun to shift. As formal judiciary systems took shape, judges built up a body of precedent that leaned toward caveat emptor, or "let the buyer beware"; under this code, buyers were not entitled to receive compensation for any problem short of outright fraud on the part of the vendor, unless the vendor had explicitly guaranteed the item. In 1534, an English judge stated: "If a man sells an unsound horse or unsound wine it behoveth that he warrant the wine to be good and the horse to be sound, otherwise the action will not lie. For if he sell the wine or horse without such warranty, it is at the other's peril and his eyes and his taste ought to be his judges in that case."[2] Records show that similar attitudes prevailed in the next century, as when an English judge ruled in 1603 that the buyer of a worthless mineral sold for its healing properties was out of luck.

Caveat emptor ruled in U.S. courts and communities as well up through the first half of the nineteenth century, and vendors rarely supplemented buyers' meager rights with any sort of formal guarantee on their wares. But to most Americans, such formalities would not have been particularly relevant anyway because products were typically produced and sold locally by people known to the buyer—often by neighbors. Ordinarily, they would have expressed their dissatisfaction on a personal basis, and word of mouth would have been more than sufficient to inform potential buyers of the quality of a particular producer's goods or of a vendor's trustworthiness.

By the 1850s, however, a new phenomenon was emerging: Many products were being sold as regional and even national brands, and department stores were opening up in the cities. The quality of national brands was often higher—and the price lower—than it was for locally manufactured counterparts; and the allure of browsing through a huge variety of items in an elegant setting was irresistible to many. But these opportunities raised questions for purchasers: What could they do if the product turned out to be flawed or otherwise unsatisfactory? Instead of dealing with a familiar face, the buyer would be confronting a corporation in another part of the country or unknown clerks in a huge store miles away.

A New Role for Guarantees

It was into this vacuum that Cyrus McCormick and John Wanamaker leapt with their money-back guarantees. Their gestures
were bold but well thought out. After all, both were selling
high-quality items to customers who were used to products of
somewhat uneven caliber, and who had better things to do
with their money than to invest it in reapers or suits only to
return these items when the whimsy passed. The gamble paid
off: Business boomed, overwhelming the costs of the occasional
return.

The lesson was not lost on American business. In 1887,
Montgomery Ward offered a money-back guarantee with its
catalog, and within a year Richard Sears had tacked a guarantee onto his watch and jewelry catalog. By the turn of the
century, guarantees from manufacturers and retailers were
becoming quite common. This trend was accelerated in 1906
with the passage of the Pure Food and Drug Act, which
required food and drug manufacturers to assure the nature
and purity of their ingredients.

Although many of these guarantees did not specify exactly
what compensation the customer could expect or under what
conditions it would be paid, and thus may have been of
dubious value, some were extremely impressive even by today's standards, essentially taking the form of an unconditional
guarantee of satisfaction. Among the many examples of guarantee payouts listed by one 1917 marketing book are a catalog
house that sent a customer a $16.50 rifle when the $11.75 rifle
he had ordered was out of stock; a department store that not
only refunded a customer's money for yard goods when the
customer later decided that she didn't like the color after
having made the material into a dress, but paid the dressmak-
er's bill as well; and a mail order house that sent replacement
leather chairs for two that had arrived with small tears, and
told the customer to have the original chairs repaired and then
to keep them.

This same book goes on to describe how some merchants
actively solicited opportunities to refund money. There was,
for example, a druggist who took down the name and phone

number of every one of his customers and then called them a week later to ask if there were any problems, encouraging them to come in for a refund if there were. There was a Maine shoe merchant (possibly L. L. Bean) whose employees would keep an eye out for customers on the street, and upon detecting the slightest sign of wear in the shoes a customer had purchased would insist that the customer return to the store to pick up a free replacement pair. And there was the Iowa jeweler who would not even discuss the possibility of exchanging merchandise with customers who had come in for that purpose; he would insist on refunding the full purchase price from his cash register, and then tell the customer that if he really wanted to buy something else in the store, he was certainly now free to do so.[3]

Such largesse was the exception rather than the rule, but the trend was clearly toward protecting the customer. Manufacturers began to follow retailers in this regard. In the 1920s the Art Metal Construction Company not only guaranteed the fireproof capabilities of its safe with a twenty-year replacement offer, but included an insurance company policy covering any losses due to the safe's failure during a burglary. Boxes of Happiness Candy came with a slip of paper stating the following: "Any box of Happiness Candy that isn't as good as *you* think it ought to be will be replaced free—and promptly and gladly."[4]

Most companies found the marketing impact of their guarantee programs well worth the trouble. The Herbert & Huesgen Company in New York offered a six-month replacement guarantee for its pens that specifically included misuse and negligence on the part of the owner; the company blissfully reported in 1924 that while the guarantee had boosted sales significantly, less than 0.01 percent of the pens had been returned. Around the same time, Hoover managed to get a little extra mileage out of its vacuum cleaner guarantees by requiring buyers to fill out a warranty card—a card that thoughtfully provided several lines on which the buyer was encouraged to list the names of vacuumless friends who might be interested in a sales call.

Guarantee Regulation

Inevitably, impressive-sounding guarantees came to be offered by small, less-than-top-quality manufacturers who had no intention of making good on them. When reputable watch manufacturers took to stamping time guarantees such as "10 years" on their watch cases, for example, fly-by-night watchmakers were soon outdoing one another in stamping longer and longer times, until the stamp "25 years" on a watch became recognized by sophisticated buyers as a sure sign of shoddy construction. (Besides, even a company making quality watches wasn't likely to be around twenty-five years later.) Shortly after the turn of the century, tire manufacturers had started offering guarantees similar in nature to those in effect today; but when the market became deluged in the next few decades by hundreds of tire manufacturers hawking disingenuous guarantees, a tire guarantee of any sort actually became associated with lack of quality, and the major tire manufacturers temporarily steered away from them.

Partly in response to such dishonest practices, the 1920s also saw the emergence of so-called third-party guarantors, such as Underwriters Laboratory, an insurance-company-sponsored organization that tested electrical appliances; the Good Housekeeping Institute, operated by *Good Housekeeping* magazine, which tested household goods; the Priscilla Proving Plant, run by *The Modern Priscilla* magazine; and the Tribune Institute, operated by the *New York Herald Tribune*. Seals of approval from any of these organizations often served to reassure customers of the basic serviceability of a product as well as of the credibility of a manufacturer's own guarantee.

Although laws governing the sale of goods were set by the states, the federal government attempted to influence these laws and make them consistent by setting forth suggested codes and encouraging the states to adopt them. Congress enacted several versions of such a code in the 1930s, most notably the Uniform Sales Act, but it wasn't until 1952 and the Uniform Commercial Code that states came into line. Adopted by all the states except Louisiana (which has a substantially different legal tradition), the Uniform Commercial Code (UCC), which is still applicable today, specifies the obligations of manufacturers and vendors with regard to "express" (explicit) and "implied" warranties. The UCC dictates that in the case of express warranties the products will:

1. Conform to any affirmation of fact made by the seller to the buyer. [For example, "The goods are 100 percent wool."]
2. Conform to any promise made by the seller to the buyer. [For example, "The color will not fade."]
3. Conform to any description of them.
4. Conform to any sample of them.

In the case of implied warranties—that is, guarantees considered to be in effect whether or not the seller has offered one—the code states that goods must be reasonably fit for the ordinary purposes for which such goods are used and that they must be of at least average quality. Furthermore, the code holds vendors responsible for misleading customers into buying a product for a use for which the product is not well-suited. Thus, under the code, vendors would be held responsible for selling a grossly inferior paint or for selling an interior paint to a customer who wanted to paint the exterior of his or her house. Finally, the code holds vendors responsible when they do not adhere to a well-recognized industry custom. If, for example, a car dealer were to deliver a car without ensuring that there was enough oil in the engine, he would be held responsible.

In addition to Congress's regulatory efforts, the Federal Trade Commission (FTC) took a stand in the 1940s on explicit guarantees, insisting that guarantees should be honored according to the way in which a consumer is likely to interpret their wording rather than according to the way in which a vendor intended them to be understood. Furthermore, the FTC said that guarantees were not fair unless they specified exactly what they covered and exactly what the customer would receive if the covered conditions were not satisfied.

This federal intervention made weak or vague guarantees obsolete. There was little marketing advantage to be gained from a guarantee that offered short-term protection from manufacturing defects, since the UCC already provided such protection. And under the FTC policy, a nonspecific claim such as "fully guaranteed" was deemed unfair. The regulation served to reduce some of the clutter among guarantee claims and made it easier for manufacturers to compete on the basis of stronger, more credible guarantees. Thus tire manufacturers again began to offer guarantees in the 1950s. A few companies even guaranteed their tires against any and all failures, including nails and other "road hazards," and one manufacturer of snow tires offered to pay to tow the cars of customers who got stuck in the snow—protection that surpasses what is offered with any of today's tires. Meanwhile, the Benrus Watch Co., after determining through surveys that the public wouldn't trust a ten-year guarantee, offered a three-year unconditional guarantee; the company credited the guarantee with turning around a five-year sales slump, and reported that watch returns ran at a modest one percent of sales.[5]

Beginnings of the Quality Link

The 1960s saw the emergence of a very loose tie between the offering of guarantees and the monitoring of customer satisfaction: It became a widespread practice among manufacturers to ask customers to mail in warranty cards with their names and addresses and then to employ the resulting information in occasional surveys of a small percentage of customers. "A manufacturer . . . should undertake frequent measurements (every six to 12 months) to discover the extent of satisfaction or dissatisfaction for his products," cautioned one 1968 marketing text. "A few hundred of these responses from customers will indicate to a manufacturer a consistent pattern of satisfaction or dissatisfaction with his products, with the service given to the products, and the combination of performance and service."[6] As we shall see in later chapters, manufacturers following this advice were just touching on a far more powerful means of linking guarantees with customer satisfaction.

By the beginning of the 1980s some businesses started to

realize that they might be missing some significant opportunities in the use of guarantees. A survey carried out for the FTC in 1977 revealed that while 40 percent of the nearly 8,000 respondents described themselves as less than "very satisfied" with their purchase of any of a wide range of products, less than 10 percent said that their problems were covered by the product's guarantee. And though about one-third of those who had had their products repaired or replaced under warranty were still not satisfied, two-thirds of these disgruntled customers never made a second attempt to have their problems addressed. Furthermore, less than 30 percent of those surveyed reported having read the warranty before making their purchase.[7] This was despite the fact that the federal Magnuson-Moss Warranty Act of 1974 had required manufacturers to make written guarantees simpler and clearer.

Throughout the 1980s many manufacturers attempted to bolster their guarantees in response to the growing obsession of the market with quality. The time coverage of guarantees in the electronics, auto, and appliance industries, for example, in many cases crept up from one year to five years, although the types of problems covered by such extended guarantees were often limited. However, it was the service sector—which began in the 1980s to rival manufacturing as a driving force of the U.S. economy, and which had also started to focus on quality—that first recognized that there was a qualitatively different way in which guarantees could be employed to significant advantage.

Although service companies had rarely employed formal guarantees, the best organizations in many types of services had long practiced a policy of attempting to do whatever it took to ensure customer satisfaction. Most consumers would be surprised, for example, if a high-priced restaurant refused to take back a steak that hadn't been properly cooked, or if a top-notch hotel refused to transfer a guest out of a room with faulty plumbing. Some service firms, then, asked themselves an obvious question: Why not put a strong guarantee in writing and try to obtain some marketing benefit from it? Most of those that did this found that something totally unexpected was taking place: The guarantees were changing the companies from top to bottom.

The guarantee had found a new incarnation—one that could apply to almost any type of organization, or even to any part of an organization.

Notes

1. Thomas Aquinas, *Summa Theologica*, Ethicus II, Question LXXVII, Article 4.
2. Sir Anthony, FitzHerbert, *The New Natura Brevium* (London: H. Lintot, 1755), p. 94C.
3. *How to Keep Business at Home* (Des Moines: *Merchants Trade Journal*, 1917).
4. Robert E. Ramsay, *Constructive Merchandising* (New York: D. Appleton & Co., 1925), p. 91.
5. *Business Week*, January 16, 1960, p. 92.
6. Richard Graves and Allan Campbell, *Creating Customers* (London: George Allen and Unwin, 1968), p. 36.
7. *Warranties Rules Consumer Baseline Study Final Report*, conducted by Arthur Young & Co. and published March 2, 1979.

Chapter 3

Why Offer an Extraordinary Guarantee?

Between 1988 and 1991, Oakley Millwork, a Chicago supplier of milled wood and other products to the regional housing construction industry, experienced a sales increase of 33 percent. That's a respectable record for almost any company, but for Oakley it was near-miraculous: During that same period, housing starts in its area fell 41 percent, and Oakley's sales, like those of its competitors, had always mirrored housing-start trends. But this time Oakley's fortunes had rocketed, even while its competitors experienced a severe downturn.

Why the sales jump? Only one significant change had preceded the turnaround: In 1988, the company initiated a "no backorder guarantee"; that is, if any item ordered from its catalog wasn't in stock and available for immediate delivery, the customer would get the item for free (see Figure 3-1).

Oakley's guarantee falls into a class that could be called *extraordinary*, meaning that it went beyond industry standards, beyond what its competitors were doing, beyond what customers had ever thought to demand, and even beyond what the company itself at first thought was feasible. By offering to provide even slightly inconvenienced customers with compensation of significant value, the company was risking its own bottom line to make a statement about its commitment to satisfying the customer.[1]

Clearly, the program had a powerful effect on sales. In its first year, $1 million of the $5 million Oakley took in revenues came from customers who specifically said that they gave

Figure 3-1. In its first year, Oakley Millwork's guarantee created $1 million in sales.

Source: Ad courtesy of Oakley Millwork.

Oakley their business because of the guarantee. And the program had an even bigger impact on profits: For the first time, the company did not have to lower its margins to cope with the price-cutting among competitors that always breaks out in a housing downturn.

But the guarantee program did far more than attract customers. It transformed the company. Since the inception of the program, Oakley has streamlined its operations, slashing costs and improving service. The company has boosted the number of times it completely turns over its inventory—a key measure of efficiency—from 4.2 to 5.8 times a year. In 1990, the company needed to purchase 15 percent of its items as more expensive special orders from distributors to avoid running out of stock; now it purchases only 8 percent as special orders. And where the company used to run an average of three special delivery runs a day to ship back-ordered items, at an annual cost of $78,000, Oakley now makes virtually no backorder deliveries.

Why a Guarantee Can Make the Difference

All this may seem like a lot to attribute to a guarantee, but the power of a guarantee to radically change an organization stems from a simple fact: If an organization has to pay in hard dollars for its mistakes, the cost of poor quality becomes unbearable. The company then has three choices: Fix the problems, go out of business, or get rid of the guarantee. Assuming that the guarantee wasn't ill-advised to begin with—which, as we shall see, is no small consideration—most companies would wisely opt to fix their problems, and would discover in the process that the guarantee provides not only the motivation but some of the means for doing so.

The concept of an extraordinary guarantee isn't a new one. As we have seen in the previous chapter, retailers and manufacturers were offering guarantees that went above and beyond the call a hundred years ago. For decades, tool purchasers have been impressed and influenced by the lifetime guarantee offered on Sears' Craftsman tools; in fact, it is common for consumers today to cite these tools as the bright exception to what is often perceived as Sears' generally moribund private-label product line. But though it is well recognized that an impressive guarantee can help a product's image and sales, such guarantees have generally been offered only with products that were of exceptionally high quality to begin with (putting aside for the moment the disingenuous use of guarantees by less reputable firms). Almost ignored has been the possibility that extraordinary guarantees can actually *produce* quality. In fact, as a number of service firms and manufacturers have clearly proved over the past few years, they can.

Although the long-term effect of guarantees on quality should ultimately prove more important to an organization's sales than the short-term direct sales effect, that's not to say that extraordinary guarantees aren't superb marketing tools. It is in the realm of marketing that guarantees provide the most immediate and visible payoff, and it is this payoff that attracts organizations to guarantees in the first place. For these reasons, we'll examine this area first, discussing general marketing benefits to start with, then looking at marketing benefits specific to service, professional service, and manufacturing companies. Next we'll discuss the more profound effect of guarantees on the way these companies operate. Finally, we'll examine some of the drawbacks to guarantees.

Boosting Market Share With Extraordinary Guarantees

In the most superficial sense, a strong guarantee can be seen as just another marketing spiel—something sellers say to buyers to convince them to make a purchase. But there is at least one substantial difference between guarantees and other marketing tools: Guarantees are legally binding contracts that can turn around and bite the offerer. A powerful guarantee can, if invoked by enough customers, have a substantial negative impact on a company's bottom line. This intimidating downside wouldn't make sense if there wasn't a powerful upside.

The most obvious element of this upside is that a strong guarantee lowers a customer's estimation of the risk of making a purchase. If customers can get their money back, for example, then they don't stand to lose as much if the transaction goes sour. In many cases, that added security has proved sufficient to convince a hesitant customer to forge ahead.

An extraordinary guarantee can also help differentiate a company from its competitors and in the process grab a significant amount of attention. The 30-day, 1,500-mile money-back guarantee offered by General Motors' Saturn subsidiary with its new cars was extensively discussed in the press, helping to establish an otherwise nonextraordinary product (at least at first glance) entering a crowded market. This sort of guarantee-based differentiation is likely to work only if a company is the first in its industry to offer an extraordinary guarantee of its type. Thus, while Chrysler, Ford, and General Motors in recent years have been continually adding to the time and mileage duration of their warranties in an effort to claim warranty superiority, only the leader of each extension has drawn considerable attention from customers. Moreover, it is easy to see, based on Saturn's approach, that significant guarantee elements were being missed by their tradition-bound competitors.

Companies looking to position themselves as producers of high-quality products and services—a near-universal desire in view of buyers' increasing impatience with unreliability—are almost certain to help their cause with an extraordinary guarantee. Such a guarantee will be perceived as a promise not to disappoint, and focuses the customer's attention on a company's commitment to quality. Many customers will reason that if a company hadn't already achieved a high level of quality, it wouldn't be able to offer an extraordinary guarantee. The guarantee must be perceived as powerful and credible, however; it must be the centerpiece of an organization's commitment to quality, not just a marketing campaign.

The appeal to customers in this case does not lie with the fact that they will be compensated if the product or service fails; rather, customers are swayed in the first place because the guarantee convinces them that the product or service won't fail. After all, getting one's money back rarely covers the true cost to a customer of poor quality; the customer has spent time buying, consuming, and then complaining about the product or service, and may have been seriously inconvenienced by its failure. Military purchasers of Texas Instruments' High-Speed Anti-Radar (HARM) missiles would surely not be satisfied with getting their money back for a missile that failed to detonate; the fact that TI guarantees that this product will perform above the specs to which it was originally contracted is meant to convince buyers that the missile will work right the first time. Guarantee-based positioning is particularly well-suited to companies that have achieved high quality but that have not yet won a reputation for quality in their market.

An extraordinary guarantee also means, of course, that if a product or service does fail, the company will do more than the usual to try to make it up to the unlucky customer. Assuming that the guarantee is backed by a solid recovery program, the guarantee will give the company a good shot at retaining a customer's business even when that customer has been victimized by a failure. As buyers become more sophisticated and the media become more cluttered with advertisements, companies are increasingly dependent on repeat and word-of-mouth business. The compensation provided to customers by a strong guarantee can go a long way toward stemming the potential loss of critical business resulting from occasional failures.

Consider the failure recovery offered by the upscale department store chain Nordstrom, famous for its willingness to bend over backwards for slighted customers. As related by Tom Peters in *Thriving On Chaos*, one business traveler customer, whose suit alterations hadn't been finished as promised before he was obliged to leave the city, arrived at the hotel at his next stop to find that the store had expressed-shipped his suits to him, along with a free set of expensive ties.[2] Such efforts constitute a costly way of winning and retaining customers, but for many businesses they are of unmatched effectiveness.

Indeed, it could be argued that an impressive failure recovery is a more powerful marketing tool than having no failure to begin with. Such were the findings of IBM's Rochester, Minnesota, plant, developer and manufacturer of the AS/400 and winner of the 1990 Malcolm Baldrige National Quality Award. As shown in Figure 3-2, IBM-Rochester undertook to chart the

Figure 3–2. Impact of recovery on retention.

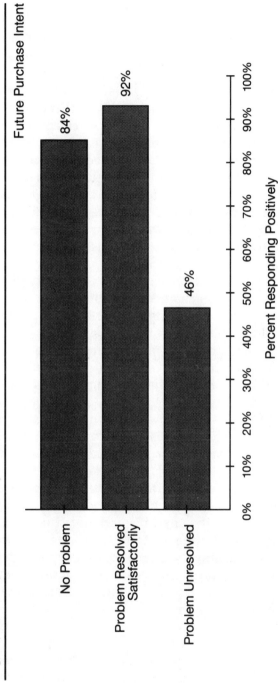

Source: IBM–Rochester study.

impact of recovery on customer retention. Its study found that customers were even more likely to bring in repeat business if a problem was resolved satisfactorily than if there had been no problem in the first place.

It is obvious that if unhappy customers are to be appeased, they must first make a complaint. Yet another study found that while return business from unhappy customers is directly dependent on how effectively the recovery is handled, the worst-case scenario is when dissatisfied customers fail to complain. Only 9 percent of unhappy customers of larger purchases will buy from the offending vendor again, whereas if the customer complains and the matter is quickly resolved, 82 percent of these customers will return. What's more, the same study found that half of all dissatisfied customers do not complain at all.

Getting feedback from customers is key. Hampton Inn, an economy-priced hotel chain known for its outstanding quality and service, invites its guests' opinions by reminding them of the chain's 100 percent satisfaction guarantee through signs in the lobby and notice cards in each room (see Figure 3-3). It knows that a complaint is often the opportunity to increase retention and that it may therefore have a positive long-term economic impact, even if in the short term a guest gets a night in the hotel free. Hence recovery payouts are not expenses and shouldn't be counted as such: They are rather marketing investments or investments in the organization's good reputation.

Finally, it is worth noting that because many customers feel that offering a strong guarantee is simply a more ethical way to do business, they may be more disposed to do business with a company offering a strong guarantee for this reason alone. Indeed, the employees of a company may well feel better about working for an organization that stands unequivocally behind the products or services it produces and that protects its customers. In addition, it is more enjoyable for employees to interact with happy customers. The literature on business ethics rarely touches on this simple point: If you don't give your customers what they paid for, you shouldn't get paid.

It seems clear that an extraordinary guarantee program *can*

Figure 3-3. Hampton Inn's ad appeared in *USA Today*, *Sports Illustrated*, and *U.S. News & World Report*.

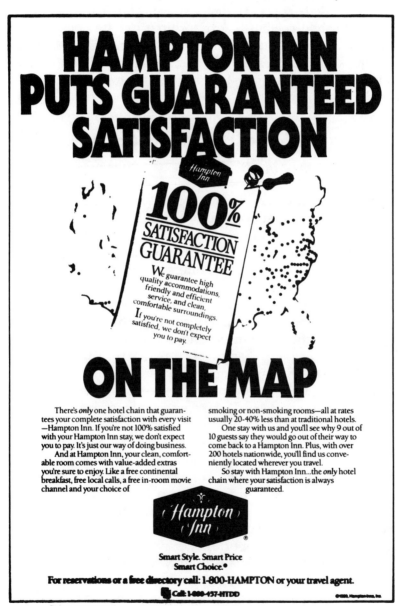

Source: © 1990 Hampton Inns, Inc.

provide a company with a competitive edge in marketing. But is it sustainable? There are many indications that it is. Companies such as Rolls Royce, Federal Express, and Sears' Craftsman tools established celebrated extraordinary guarantees early in their histories, and have continued to earn mileage off the guarantees year after year. In general, perceptions of high quality—or of low quality—take a long time to wear off.

How Guarantees Help Service Companies Win Customers

Service companies, which now account for 80 percent of the GNP, have the greatest opportunity to differentiate themselves through offering a guarantee. One reason for this is that service industries (excluding retailers, which serve as agents for manufacturers) traditionally haven't offered formal guarantees. Unlike manufacturers' products, their offerings aren't covered by warranty law, and customers generally have not learned to expect a guarantee. Thus a service company that offers any sort of meaningful guarantee—and, as we shall see, there are many ways to offer meaningless guarantees—is essentially offering an extraordinary guarantee.

It is not merely tradition that has kept service companies from offering guarantees. There are several reasons why doing so presents a special challenge to service companies. With products, the source of customer dissatisfaction has traditionally been clear-cut, typically stemming from a demonstrable defect or lack of functionality. For example, if light bulbs don't work, customers know that they can return them. On the service side, the root of dissatisfaction can be vague. Services are generally intangible entities that leave customers with little to use as evidence in support of a complaint. Successful delivery of the service is usually highly dependent on human performance, and people are unpredictable, inconsistent, and often hard to control. Furthermore, since the production of a service and its consumption take place at the same moment, there is no opportunity to inspect the service after production in order to catch and correct errors before they are delivered to the customer.

These challenges also afford an opportunity for service companies to employ guarantees to great effect. While we expect a clock radio to be guaranteed, we would be surprised and delighted to get a guarantee of good service from our insurance companies, taxi services, or schools. With competition growing more fierce every day in most service industries and customers becoming more demanding, companies are eager for any means to differentiate themselves from competitors and overcome customer concerns about obtaining the highest value for their money. And although most service companies are continually trying to impress on customers that they strive for customer satisfaction, few efforts would communicate this commitment more effectively than a powerful guarantee underwritten by the company's senior executives. Guarantees can be especially helpful for restaurants, auto repair shops, executive search firms, advertising agencies, and other businesses that depend on referrals and that are particularly vulnerable to negative word of mouth.

For many service companies, offering a powerful guarantee may not represent much of a leap. Some have already incorporated the goal of complete customer satisfaction into their corporate philosophies: When customer problems occur, they traditionally have done whatever is necessary to resolve the problem. In that case, a guarantee may simply be a matter of formalizing the concept to increase market share and customer loyalty, to further impress on the organization's employees the concept of absolute customer satisfaction, and perhaps to improve profitability.

Guarantee Marketing at Professional Service Firms

The interest in guarantees is even beginning to seep into professional service firms such as law offices, medical practices, advertising agencies, management consultancies, and investment banking firms. Such firms typically provide very high-value, high-cost services to a relatively small number of clients;

thus the triggering of even a single money-back guarantee could be exceptionally painful.

But there are reasons why guarantees can also be of exceptional benefit to these firms, especially in winning the business of first-time buyers. First of all, fees for many types of professional service firms often run into six figures. By offering compensation for a service failure, the guarantee reduces the perceived risk and creates value for clients. In addition, the negative consequences of unsolved problems are high. Bad service from a restaurant can ruin someone's evening; bad service from a medical center or law firm can ruin someone's life. The greater the client's expected aggravation, expense, and time lost, the greater will be the power of the guarantee.

Professional services are also highly customized. The past history of the firm's performance with other buyers does not always provide a reliable indication of how the firm will do with a new project, since different customers are serviced in entirely different ways, often with different personnel assigned to each project. A guarantee can provide a strong indication of a firm's reliability.

Furthermore, marketing opportunities tend to be restricted for professional service firms, as are differentiating characteristics that can be clearly articulated to potential clients. A strong guarantee can provide such a differentiator, standing out in many potential clients' minds. How the guarantee is communicated to clients is, of course, a vital consideration.

In general, buyer resistance is high with respect to professional services. Clients tend to be extremely cautious, which leads to long and often fruitless sales efforts on the part of service producers. A guarantee is an especially effective tool for overcoming resistance and closing the sale. As one example, the advertising agency DDB Needham guaranteed its clients that it would tightly manage and reduce administrative costs up to 30 percent. In an industry where runaway costs are almost considered the norm, such a guarantee could determine whether a client signs or walks.

Guarantee Marketing by Manufacturers

Merely offering a guarantee generally has little impact on customers and potential customers of manufactured items.

After all, a certain degree of guarantee protection is required by law, and most customers fully expect to find some sort of formal warranty accompanying virtually any product they purchase. Indeed, as mentioned in Chapter 2, consumers typically don't read these warranties prior to making a purchase.

Is there any way, then, for manufacturers to derive significant marketing benefit from a guarantee? There is: They must make a special effort to come up with an *extraordinary* guarantee. They can do so in a variety of ways: by dramatically extending the time duration or scope of the warranty, as some car manufacturers have done; by offering a more-than-your-money-back guarantee, such as Speedy Muffler King's 110 percent guarantee; by making it exceptionally easy to receive the guarantee payout, as Wal-Mart stores do through not requiring receipts or any paperwork; or by offering an unconditional guarantee of satisfaction, which enables customers to return a product even if nothing whatsoever is wrong with it. (Although some retailers offer such a guarantee, a manufacturer could extend it to cover those customers who purchased the product at a store that didn't.) Book publisher William Morrow, for example, offers an unconditional money-back guarantee with the book *Future Edge* by Joel Arthur Barker. This sort of exceptional guarantee can capture the potential customer's attention and go a long way toward overcoming hesitations about buying. Consider, too, the impact that the mere prospect of offering a guarantee can have on the book's quality!

Jolting Operations Through Extraordinary Guarantees

The dynamics of offering a well-thought-out extraordinary guarantee are such that guarantees become more than a promise of quality; they become a source of it. They do so by providing a steady stream of detailed customer feedback on problem areas and by simultaneously applying an unpleasant shock to the corporate bottom line if quality is below par. In other words, guarantees can make companies aware of what's wrong and motivate them to fix it. While the Malcolm Baldrige National Quality Award framework acts as a catalyst in organizing and systematizing changes, the extraordinary guarantee is a driver at the core of all total quality management activities. It can be used to turn up the pressure, and as in turning up the pressure on a garden hose, the leaks become more apparent. Organizations that are unwilling or unable to take advantage of these benefits would do best to stay away from offering extraordinary guarantees, regardless of the marketing benefits that might accrue. If their higher-quality competitors offer extraordinary guarantees, however, their dilemma is obvious. In this regard, they need to use the extraordinary guarantee concept as a lightning rod, as a galvanizing force for organization-wide quality improvement.

Many companies that do without extraordinary guarantees believe they already have a good flow of customer feedback through conventional complaint-gathering channels or through market research. Although companies usually recognize that not all dissatisfied customers complain, they insist that they can get a good handle on the extent of customer dissatisfaction simply by assuming that each complaint represents some larger number of dissatisfied customers—say, ten—who didn't complain. But whatever multiplier a company picks to amplify actual complaints, it is likely to seriously underestimate the degree of customer dissatisfaction with some aspects of the product or service and perhaps miss others altogether. Take the case related by one executive of an ill-fated Pan Am flight on which, after a lengthy delay, the passengers were switched to another plane, the flight was then canceled, and the baggage of every stranded passenger was lost: Out of a plane full of people, not one complained to Pan Am. Most likely, no one felt that it was worth the effort. That's a lot of missed data points.

Part of the problem is that getting a complaint through to the right person in a company—that is, someone in a position to act on the information—can be an arduous process, a process that the great majority of consumers see as providing only a modest chance of resolving the problem and virtually no chance of engendering meaningful change at the company. It is entirely possible, and probably common, for a company to irritate millions of customers without a single complaint getting through to a manager capable of doing something about the problem. Some companies take special pains to solicit comments by leaving comment cards in hotel rooms, for example, or by having waiters ask diners if everything is all right. But these efforts generally do little to overcome the customer's belief that complaining is unpleasant and a waste of time.

Likewise, market research alone may not provide an accurate picture of customer problems. Such research provides a snapshot of customer perceptions obtained under artificial conditions—perhaps long after the customer has forgotten about his or her bad experience—and can't by itself hope to keep up with the dynamics of complex, rapidly changing market environments. Customer preferences and standards are constantly changing, but market research is static. One need only look at the disastrous introduction of "New Coke"—backed up by one of the most extensive state-of-the-art market research programs in the history of business—to see the potential weaknesses of this approach.

On the other hand, an exceptional guarantee program not only invites complaints, it rewards them. Provided with a strong incentive to make themselves heard, customers in effect become quality inspectors for the company, continually measuring and reporting on the success of the company's efforts. Confronted with a significant volume of complaints, and the threat of profit erosion associated with guarantee payouts, a company has little choice but to shift its focus from business as usual to serving the customer—and not just paying lip service to serving the customer, but actually doing whatever it takes to make customers satisfied and to minimize their demand for payouts.

Achieving this sort of all-consuming customer focus tends to be extremely difficult for U.S. companies. That's one of the main keys to the success achieved by Japanese companies, which speak of the customer not as king, but as God. Toyota salesmen in Japan, for example, routinely attend the funerals of customers and their families. U.S. companies need to become equally obsessed with customer satisfaction to compete, and guarantees provide one way of ensuring that obsession. Furthermore, guarantees force companies to translate that obsession into operational changes that are relevant to customer satisfaction. That was the case at Oakley Millwork, which forced itself to learn exactly which inventory controls would enable it to avoid backorders. If Oakley had started to slip, it would have been immediately burdened with guarantee payouts, requiring rapid adjustment. There is no room for backsliding, a common problem with companies that have implemented quality programs.

An appropriately designed extraordinary guarantee forces internal operational changes. Specifically, it requires an organization to explicitly define its customers' needs and to understand its manufacturing and service delivery process, including controllable and uncontrollable variables as well as possible failure points and weaknesses in the system. A strong guarantee also requires an organization to establish customer-satisfaction measures as key performance indicators and to track errors, establishing—and making work—a feedback loop for continual improvement. Finally, a guarantee gives a sense of urgency to this process, forcing organizations to focus all their resources on succeeding.

Energizing Employees

There is yet another dimension to the effect guarantees can have on a company's operations: They can motivate employees to achieve unprecedented levels of performance. Eliminating customer dissatisfaction is a goal very different from the ordinary incentives and threats of the corporate world. Like a sports team in a playoff game, an organization can be energized by the raised stakes and the unusually high level of performance that is being asked of it. An extraordinary guarantee can provide a sense of mission and a feeling that each employee's actions count for something. If employees at all levels know that their actions can prevent a customer from demanding a payout, then they feel that they are in a position to contribute directly to the bottom line and that they are responsible for meeting the standards by which the company measures its success.

A good example of this effect occurred at Marriott's Desert Springs Resort. A meeting planner representing a teachers' association that wanted to hold its conference at the resort was discouraged upon learning that Marriott's regional senior executive meeting was scheduled to take place there at the same time. It seemed obvious to him that when quality service was being portioned out, the executives would win out over the teachers. When he said he would look elsewhere, Marriott's sales manager replied, "What if I guarantee that if for any reason your clients are dissatisfied, we will not charge you?" The meeting planner said, "Put it in writing." The sales manager did. The word went out that the great news for the Desert Springs Resort was that the teachers' association would be in town for Labor Day, but the bad news was the guarantee. However, the resort's general manager brought the department managers together and said, "Let's make this work." Problems that had defied solutions for years evaporated over night. Working as a team energized by the high stakes involved, individual employees reached new performance levels in their zeal to do whatever it took to satisfy both groups.

Senior managers, recognizing that employees play at least as large a role as they do in avoiding guarantee-related disasters, will have a far greater interest in ensuring that employees are empowered to keep customers satisfied. Because achieving the operational effectiveness demanded by a guarantee initiative requires the smooth functioning of the entire organization, the program fosters team building even across departmental walls. For instance, when Ford purchased Jaguar, guaranteeing the new division's product sent the average warranty cost soaring to the unacceptable level of $800 per car; but the division rallied, jumped on the problems, and improved Jaguar's quality. A company that has put its own profits on the line to strongly guarantee the satisfaction of every single customer simply has no room for parochialism, territoriality, or routine.

Routine went by the wayside when it was found that it took too long to deliver pizzas at the Marriott Bethesda and guarantee payouts started to mount. A scrutiny of the service determined that the hotel's elevators were simply too slow. To avoid the bottleneck, room-service people were outfitted with track shoes and were encouraged to run up and down the stairs. By its very novelty and risk, an extraordinary guarantee program can serve as a jolt that snaps people out of operating on autopilot. Any employees representing weak links will be quickly identified and set straight; if not, quality problems will slip between the cracks and result in guarantee payouts. The company must get everyone on board or risk drowning. This can be accomplished without using the guarantee as a club. When employees are asked, "What would have to change in your area for you to feel that you could be a strong link in the guaranteed chain of quality?" their enthusiasm is invariably fired.

Don't the operational improvements associated with an extraordinary guarantee program, like most quality programs, come at some significant cost? Paradoxically, a good guarantee program almost always *lowers* operational costs in the long term, as it did at Oakley Millwork. Ensuring customer satisfaction while under the gun of guarantee payouts means getting everything done right the first time and providing employees with the training and tools to do it. As an organization works harder and smarter to achieve this goal, it may find that it can cut down on rework and inspection and increase production. Significant cost savings start to emerge, even though they were not the motivation for the efforts. Moveover, guarantee-induced improvements make organizations better places in which to work. By contrast, companies undertaking traditional quality improvement programs often end up involving more people in their problem solving. They create improvements, yes, but raise costs as well.

How Service Companies Benefit

Because quality in service industries tends to be subjective, service companies are again well positioned to take advantage of the benefits inherent in extraordinary guarantees. A service company that can break out of the large circle of mediocre performers that dominate many service industries is likely to have a large impact on the market. And an extraordinary guarantee program can help it break out of that sea of muddy mediocrity and into the limelight.

Serious quality improvement efforts are often lacking at service companies, especially multisite service companies with many small outlets scattered about. The problem is not that managers consciously skimp on quality but rather that managers end up providing service levels that meet their own standards of effectiveness instead of aiming for the more challenging service levels associated with complete customer satisfaction. It's difficult enough to operate a multisite service company, especially if it involves franchises. Creating a world-class multisite service operation is a huge challenge. An extraordinary guarantee counters this pressure by providing local customers with an incentive to complain and thus forcing managers to face service shortcomings.

A strong guarantee can help guard against the occasional tendency at service companies to attempt to service too many customers in relation to the resources available. Manufacturing companies can't deliver half-finished products and thus are forced to ask their customers to wait for production to catch up with demand. Service companies, on the other hand, can be tempted to skimp on service so as to maximize income. An obvious example of this skimping is seen when a few waiters vainly try to serve a crowded restaurant. A strong guarantee would make that practice an exceedingly dangerous one.

At professional service firms in particular, a guarantee can reduce the temptation to overpromise during the selling effort, since the firm will be held fully accountable for any promises it makes. A guarantee forces open and honest dialogue with clients, leading to a precise definition of client needs and expectations and of the firm's service system capabilities.

How Manufacturers Benefit

Manufacturing companies have made tremendous efforts over the past decade to strengthen quality. Unfortunately, these efforts have not always paid off. According to *The Wall Street*

Journal, over half the quality improvement programs under-taken by companies in recent years have been abandoned or scaled back out of dissatisfaction and disappointment.[3]

Why might an exceptional guarantee program succeed where other programs have failed? Because guarantees place quality improvement in a new context: The company has to improve quality not simply because managers are telling every-one that it's a good idea, but because if the quality problems result in dissatisfied customers, the company will immediately start losing significant amounts of money in payouts. Poor quality also results in losses at companies that don't offer exceptional guarantees, of course, but in a fashion that doesn't point so directly to the particular problems that are most responsible for customer irritation. To this day, executives at American auto manufacturers talk about their Japanese com-petitors' "100-mile" advantage, which refers to the fact that Japanese cars on average have fewer minor problems, such as the trim popping off, in the first weeks after sale. In focusing on such relatively minor (though obviously not insignificant) quality issues, U.S. car companies allowed themselves to be-come largely indifferent to the more fundamental problems— such as poor long-term reliability and inferior design—that caused them to lose market share to the Japanese. How would the U.S. car companies' approach have changed if they had offered unconditional guarantees on their cars in the 1970s?

Internal Guarantees

The exact same benefits that accrue to companies offering exceptional guarantees to customers can accrue to divisions, departments, or groups that offer guarantees to their internal customers. Such guarantees can serve as one of the means of meeting the improved operational quality demands imposed by the external guarantees offered customers. As we'll see in more detail in Chapter 7, internal guarantees can also get at some problem areas, such as hiring practices and the produc-tivity of meetings, that even an external guarantee might not reach.

In addition, internal guarantees can serve as a form of

training and education for a company that is considering implementing an external guarantee; many of the same issues will arise, but the cost of errors will be (at least from a corporate bottom line point of view) nearly zero. Even if a company decides not to implement an external guarantee, it may choose to retain internal guarantees for their effect on some areas of quality.

Drawbacks of Extraordinary Guarantees

The greatest risk of an extraordinary guarantee program is that it will be poorly prepared for or carelessly implemented. If the company turns out to be unable or unwilling to improve quality, an unending stream of guarantee payouts could result. It's not impossible that the marketing benefits of the guarantee will outweigh the cost of payouts. Some of the manufacturers of the bizarre, shoddy products advertised on late night cable television clearly count on customer inertia (or on having left the state) to avoid having to pay out extensively on their extravagant guarantees. But for most companies, this is an unwise risk indeed.

Some companies are simply so lacking in quality from the start that even a valiant, guarantee-driven effort to improve would produce positive results too slowly to enable them to withstand the torrent of payouts that would flow out in the meantime. In garden hose imagery, if turning up the pressure on a quality organization makes leaks more apparent, turning it up on an organization lacking in quality could well rupture the hose or blow out the valve. Moreover, employees may lose respect for executive management's judgment. Many of the low-end electronics companies such as Emerson Electronics that dabbled in the low-end personal computer market ended up withdrawing not only because of poor sales but also because the cost of maintaining even industry-standard one-year warranties proved burdensome on their low-quality products. Issuing an extraordinary guarantee would have been a thoroughly masochistic act without first getting things in order. The extraordinary guarantee *vision* would be the right place to start for such a company, followed by the question, "What would it take to implement the level of quality needed?" When implementation of the guarantee is seriously considered, it is wise to try it out first on a trusted, loyal client. The concept of the extraordinary guarantee may seem simple, but it is not an easy approach to getting the hard improvement work done.

A guarantee doesn't always help achieve quality goals and can occasionally even hinder such efforts. For example, a money-back guarantee offered by a professional service firm would not be appropriate if it fostered the perception that the onus was on the firm to pay out rather than on the firm's manager to provide quality service to begin with. When a money-back guarantee is in force, customers may feel disinclined to invoke the guarantee unless their dissatisfaction is large, commensurate with the payout. This is especially true at service companies, and even more so at professional service firms. For example, customers who are averse to confrontation or who have a strong interest in preserving their relationship with the service provider may not complain when they are unhappy with certain aspects of a firm's service—and thus will not trigger the guarantee payout. In effect, the guarantee has motivated the customer to *not* complain, a result that is precisely opposite to the desired goal of obtaining valuable information about a company's flaws for the purposes of correcting those flaws. One example: Domino's original guarantee of speedy pizza delivery stated that the pizza would be free if it wasn't there within thirty minutes; but the company discovered that many customers felt guilty about demanding a free pizza when delivery was late, thus allowing some delivery process problems to slip through the cracks. (We'll see later how Domino's fixed the problem.)

Some businesses or entire industries will want to shy away from certain unconditional guarantees because of uncontrollable factors that have large impacts on customer satisfaction. House builders, for example, are often at the whim of weather, suppliers, architects, and zoning boards and could not safely offer an on-time guarantee. Companies that are financially unstable or that depend on a few large customers, as do some small consultants, could be quickly forced into bankruptcy by a few guarantee payouts. In most of these instances, however, a company can get significant benefit from extraordinary guarantees that cover key components of their service over which they do have control.

As we'll explore in detail in a later chapter, most managers who believe cheating will pose a significant problem are underestimating their customers. But occasionally a company will have to deal with a customer base that is especially likely to take unfair advantage of guarantees, and such a company must consider limiting its generosity. Clothing retailers, for example, have long been plagued by customers who buy expensive outfits, wear them on one occasion, and then return them, having intended to do so from the beginning; a double-your-money-back guarantee would be out of place in these businesses.

When Guarantees Send the Wrong Message

Most companies find that customers don't question the credibility of a well-thought-out guarantee or the intentions behind it. However, because extraordinary guarantees are sometimes offered on shoddy products by fly-by-night outfits (such as many of the companies that sell office lighting supplies by phone), some smaller companies could occasionally encounter customers whose level of skepticism is actually raised by a strong guarantee.

A guarantee may also call attention to an otherwise little-considered potential problem with a product or service, thus hurting the chances of a sale. A guarantee that a carpet cleaner won't have an unpleasant odor, for example, could worry customers who had never previously considered the possibility of a carpet cleaner smelling bad. Especially at high-end and professional service firms, a guarantee can foster skepticism because customers may wonder why a guarantee needs stating in the first place. Sophisticated buyers usually believe they are entitled to good service and expect it from any firm with which they do business. Emphasizing a guarantee may even irritate clients who assume that they already have an implicit agreement with the provider.

A guarantee may conflict with the sophisticated, upscale image that a high-priced restaurant or a consulting firm wishes to project. It might also give the impression that a firm is begging for business. Paradoxically, an explicit guarantee can even introduce an element of doubt into customers' minds about the ability of the firm to deliver the promised level of service. Guarantees can send out a negative message: that failure is within the realm of possibility. If both quality and customers' perception of quality in an industry are unusually high, then even if a strong guarantee doesn't hurt a company's image it probably can't help it either.

In many professional service industries, presentations of guarantees that smack of tinny merchandising ("Service with a smile or $5 off the bill") or that seek to influence consumers through emotional factors not relevant to professional competence might rightly be considered undignified and thus unethical. Indeed, overt self-promotion of any sort is frowned on (though certainly not absent) in the legal and medical professions, among others. "We're not out there selling cars or underarm deodorant," noted one management consultant. "Firms like ours are perceived to be on some higher plane."

The pitfalls and drawbacks of extraordinary guarantees should not be underestimated: Most companies offering extraordinary guarantees eventually withdraw them. That doesn't mean that a strong guarantee program doesn't stand a good chance of success. These programs frequently fail because the companies offering them do not understand the relationship between guarantees and quality; or sometimes, a company simply chooses the wrong type of guarantee to offer, or fails to properly design, implement, and fine-tune the guarantee. As we'll see in the following chapters, all these errors can be avoided. If they are, most companies will find that an extraordinary guarantee can be one of the best ways to achieve excellence and break away from the competition.

Notes

1. Relevant reading on pushing service companies through the barrier between merely good and excellent quality can be found in James L. Heskett,

W. Earl Sasser, Jr., and Christopher W. L. Hart, *Service Breakthroughs: Changing the Rules of the Game* (New York: Free Press, 1990).
2. Tom Peters, *Thriving on Chaos* (New York: Alfred A. Knopf, 1987), pp. 89–90.
3. "Quality Programs Show Shoddy Results," *Wall Street Journal,* May 14, 1992, p. B1.

Chapter 4

Types of Extraordinary Guarantees

There are many types of guarantees that can be employed to powerful effect, and each has its advantages and drawbacks. In this chapter I'll define the major categories of guarantees and discuss their characteristics in broad terms. The challenge of matching a particular company's requirements to these characteristics is addressed in Chapter 5.

Nonguarantees

First, I should mention those few types of guarantees that won't be considered here, either because they can't be made extraordinary or because they can't easily be utilized to significantly improve a company's success. These lesser guarantees fall into four categories: (1) guarantees that meet minimum legal requirements; (2) guarantees for which the customer explicitly pays extra (service contracts); (3) guarantees forced on a company by a customer (nonperformance penalties); and (4) guarantees offered by third parties.

All U.S. states except Louisiana require manufacturers to protect buyers minimally with a guarantee that conforms to the Uniform Commercial Code—whether or not the manufacturer explicitly states the guarantee. As discussed earlier, the code compels manufacturers to refund the purchase price for or to repair or replace defective, substandard, or inappropriately marketed products. Because all manufacturers are bound by this guarantee, offering it can't provide a competitive advantage. And while a company offering exceptionally shabby products could obviously be forced by having to honor this minimal guarantee to raise its quality to some extent, such a minimal guarantee in itself won't motivate a company to substantially improve its operations.

A service contract is an agreement by which a company agrees to provide a customer with protection that goes beyond the ordinary warranty. Typically, the contract specifies that if the product fails, it will be repaired at little or no cost. While this contract might provide some of the same protection offered by an extraordinary guarantee, it differs in that a service contract is generally purchased by the customer as extra protection, whereas a guarantee is offered free of charge as an integral part of the product. The contract, in essence, says, "When it breaks, you don't have to pay us for the repair because you have paid us for a service contract." The guarantee says, "In the unlikely event that it breaks, we will repair it for free because we stand behind our products." Customers can reasonably assume that companies profit on their service contracts. Some elevator companies, for example, derive most of their earnings not from installing elevators but from servicing them. Thus offering a service contract says relatively little about a company's commitment to quality.

In much the same vein, there is a strong distinction that should be made between a guarantee offered by a company and a contract in which the customer requires a company to meet certain standards under threat of loss of payment or reduction of payment (or loss of future contracts). Even though the standards specified by a guarantee and a contract might be identical, they may again produce very different results. When a company provides a guarantee, it is offering to stand behind its own performance; it is a form of self-motivation, one in which the company can take pride. When a company is forced by a contract to perform under the threat of penalty, it is more likely to focus on doing what it can to meet the requirements with a minimum of extra effort, or even to subvert the intentions of the requirements to get by. Government contractors typically work under such contractual requirements rather than under voluntary guarantees, and the frequently mediocre and occasionally criminally substandard results are legendary.

Finally, third-party guarantees, such as Good Housekeeping's "Seal of Approval," and extended warranties offered by credit card companies can rarely be expected to contribute to a company's performance. As valuable as these guarantees may (or may not) be to the customer, they are essentially promises made by the third party to the customer and have little bearing on how the company providing the product or service conducts its business.

Putting aside these weaker forms of guarantees, then, let's examine some of the many ways of categorizing the types of guarantees that can turn a company around. One way to categorize them is on the basis of whether the guarantee is an external guarantee, offered by the company to its customers, or internal, offered by some group within the company to other people or groups working for the company. Although internal guarantees can look and function exactly like external guarantees, their immediate goal is to raise quality in a specific area of the company, not directly to help deliver customer satisfaction, as is the case with external guarantees. Because there is consequently a different set of considerations associated with them, we will examine internal guarantees in a separate chapter, and restrict the discussion here to external guarantees.

External guarantees can be explicit or implicit. When a company offers an explicit guarantee, it clearly states what it is promising and what it will do if it fails to keep that promise (the payout). An implicit guarantee leaves one or both of these elements unstated. That's not to say an implicit guarantee is weaker; indeed, as we shall see later, implicit guarantees can be among the strongest of all guarantees. But first, let's examine the different types of explicit guarantees.

The Unconditional Guarantee of Satisfaction

Here is L. L. Bean's guarantee, stated prominently in its catalogs, in its advertising, and near the entrance to its main store in Freeport, Maine: "Everything we sell is backed by a 100% unconditional guarantee. We do not want you to have anything from L. L. Bean that is not completely satisfactory. Return anything you buy from us at any time for any reason it proves otherwise." No loopholes, no qualifications, no room for confusion. Just return it and get your money back—for whatever reason, or even for no good reason at all, any time.

Of all the things that a company can say to its customers, an unconditional guarantee of satisfaction is perhaps the most powerful. The term itself communicates the key points of the message: "Unconditional," meaning no excuses, no explanations, no fine print; and "satisfaction," meaning that you are the final arbiter of what this company has done right and what it has done wrong.

An unconditional guarantee says, in effect, "We will meet all of your expectations." It makes absolute customer satisfaction a mission statement for how a company conducts its business. It is also the form of guarantee to which managers appear to be naturally drawn. In one consulting firm, groups of executives were asked to draft proposed guarantees. Although they varied somewhat in wording, the contents of the entries were strikingly similar: All were basically unconditional guarantees.

As powerful as they are, unconditional guarantees are also usually the simplest to state. One environmental consulting firm places the following sentence in the cover letters it includes with its proposals: "The firm unconditionally guarantees customer satisfaction or its fees need not be paid." Apparel catalog retailer Lands' End has abbreviated its unconditional guarantee in its promotional materials this way: "Guaranteed. Period." (See Figure 4-1.) Companies operating under this sort of statement are holding themselves to the highest possible standard: the customer's.

The unconditional guarantee of satisfaction is the mother of all extraordinary guarantees, amplifying all their benefits. The marketing impact can be tremendous: L. L. Bean and Lands' End both have built entire campaigns around them. The potential effect on quality is commensurately large: Whatever errors a company is making, no matter how complex or subtle,

Figure 4-1. Lands' End doesn't trumpet its guarantee in bold letters, but makes it an integral part of the quality and service message.

Duck cloth, kangaroo pockets, alligator teeth and a thing that holds your keys.

Luckily for ducks, our Lands' End Original Attache is made of 18-ounce cotton duck canvas. Duck canvas, you see, is the very same rugged material sails were once made of. So it can weather wind, rain, snow and whatever Mother Nature can throw at it.

And naturally, whatever you can throw into it.

You'll find ten pockets inside. Each of which we fastidiously stitch with durable cotton-wrapped polyester thread. Unlike ordinary threads, it won't burn up or weaken on the heavy-duty sewing machines that we use.

Nifty spaces organize checkbooks, calculators, eyeglasses, papers, pencils and other stuff that somehow always needs organizing. There is even a neat strap to keep track of keys. That's nice.

Outside, a generous pouch opens up and closes with a reinforced strip of Velcro.® (It's enough to make a marsupial envious.)

The handles are padded with a thick piece of nylon rope. While boxed "x-stitching" crosses the webbing of the grips three times.

Equally strong are hundreds of teeth carefully sewn not once, but twice, into the zipper. Our zipper's two large pull rings are shaped from a solid piece of steel. They're tough.

As with all of the items we carry, the value of our attache lies in the attention that we pay to details.

The Lands' End Original Attache, under $40.

Our Pinpoint Oxford shirts alone have to pass 71 inspections before they're passed on to you.

Whether you're looking for a classic pair of khaki trousers or a handmade quilt for your bed, you can be sure that if it's in our catalog, it is Guaranteed. Period.® Which simply means, if for any reason, no matter how small it may seem to you, you are not quite satisfied with one of our products,

send it back. What you will get in return is your money or another item. That's why we say "Period."

Everything our catalogs list represents a value and a quality that you would be hard-pressed to come across elsewhere. If you would like to see what we mean exactly, just call our friendly operators in Dodgeville at 1-800-356-4444, toll-free, any day of the week.

They'll be happy to send you a free Lands' End catalog that's filled with all sorts of quality home furnishings and comfortable clothing for men, women and children.

By the way, have you seen our fine turtlenecks?

To get our free catalog call 1-800-356-4444.

Or fill out the coupon and mail it to:
1 Lands' End Lane, Dept. HW, Dodgeville, WI 53595

Name _____

Address _____

_____ Apt _____

City _____ State _____

Zip _____ Phone (___)

Guaranteed. Period.®

© 1992 Lands' End, Inc.

Source: © 1992 Lands' End, Inc.

they are sure to come flying back in its face, instead of quietly slinking away along with ex-customers. The unconditional guarantee gives the company a chance to make good with virtually any less-than-completely-satisfied customer and to correct all sources of error so as to avoid slighting future customers.

While retailers have long been the leaders in offering unconditional guarantees of satisfaction, other types of companies have become bolder in adopting them. Service companies have been among the most adventurous. That makes sense because for service companies, satisfaction often *is* the product. Objective standards are hard to come by when considering service companies. For example, how do you measure the defects in a steak dinner, or in a public relations campaign? Thus the customer's satisfaction becomes the most important, if not always the most reliable, yardstick for quality. Guaranteeing it unconditionally is the most effective way in which a company can stand behind its service.

Unconditional guarantees of satisfaction have cropped up in a number of service industries. The Hampton Inn chain guarantees its hotel rooms; guests who say they aren't satisfied with their stay get a complete refund. Bain & Company offers some clients an unconditional guarantee on its management consulting services; one client was quoted in *The New York Times* as giving this reason for his continuing to do business with Bain: "If they fall short of performance, they don't get paid. Period."[1] Even services that have traditionally not offered any sort of guarantee are experimenting with unconditional guarantees. One example: A business professor at the University of Southern California will refund tuition and textbook costs to any student of his course who isn't completely satisfied with the course. There's one condition: They have to ask for the refund before final grades are out.

Manufacturers don't have the problem of not being able to measure quality objectively; generally speaking, it's simple to determine whether or not a product is broken. Because product failure is usually the most visible cause of customer dissatisfaction, manufacturers' warranties have always addressed defects; it has simply been assumed that if the product isn't defective, the manufacturer has done enough to ensure customer satisfaction. However, customers can have many reasons to be dissatisfied with products that are functioning normally. For example, an air conditioner could be excessively noisy, a car could have seats that feel uncomfortable on long trips, or a toothpaste's taste could be unpleasant.

A growing number of manufacturers are trying to address these more elusive elements of customer satisfaction with unconditional guarantees. General Electric offers a ninety-day unconditional guarantee on some of its large home appliances; if for any reason a customer isn't happy with the appliance, he or she can return it and receive a refund or replacement. Digital Equipment Corporation has offered a 120-day unconditional guarantee on its office computers.

The automobile industry, long a bellwether of manufacturing warranties, has begun to explore unconditional guarantees. Given the cost of a car, that's a potentially risky proposition; as a result, car companies are moving on this slowly. General Motors' Saturn division offers a thirty-day, 1,500-mile unconditional guarantee on its cars; GM's Oldsmobile division and Chrysler have both experimented with similar guarantees. These truly exceptional guarantees (unlike the extended mileage warranties) have earned the cars on which they are offered a great deal of favorable press coverage, as well as extra attention from consumers. Some dealers reported strong sales jumps when the Oldsmobile and Chrysler guarantees were rolled out, and Saturn has quickly become one of the best-selling cars in the United States.

The Risks of Unconditional Guarantees

Unconditional guarantees of satisfaction have a significant potential drawback: They can lead to a painfully high number of demands for payout. Part of the problem is that such guarantees, by definition, provide such broad coverage of a product or service that almost everyone could find *something* that might tempt them to take the company up on its generous guarantee. And a minor but easily noticeable glitch could trigger mass payout demands.

Another possible concern is the threat of unreasonable triggerings. After all, customers don't have to provide a good reason for triggering the guarantee, and in many cases they might not have one: Imagine having to take back an automobile from a customer who drove it 1,500 miles before deciding the color of the trunk carpeting was too bright, or having to refund the price of a hotel room because a guest had a bad dream. (Nevertheless, as we shall see in a later chapter, silly or fraudulent triggering almost always turns out to be a minor problem.)

Even if the customer is legitimately dissatisfied with the product or service, it may be for reasons beyond the company's control. A taxi company offering an unconditional guarantee would find itself constantly paying out over traffic jams, no matter how clean its cabs or how courteous its drivers. Of course, in some businesses uncontrollable triggerings could be avoided by working harder to manage customers' expectations during the sale, and scrupulously avoiding oversell. In fact, such actions could be considered yet another form of quality control motivated by the guarantee. A company might even find itself reexamining the question of what is uncontrollable: An airline that constantly paid out on an unconditional guarantee because of weather delays might start to come up with creative ways of keeping customers happy when such delays occur—providing them with special snacks and extra drinks, for example, or allowing free use of airphones.

Despite such efforts, companies offering unconditional guarantees will inevitably find themselves occasionally paying out on them under outrageous conditions. One can only imagine how many pairs of boots L. L. Bean has replaced for free after owners have gotten years of comfortable wear out of them. These costs must be weighed against the exceptional benefits of unconditional guarantees of satisfaction. But some managers, even after recognizing the tremendous marketing, quality, and customer retention advantages of these guarantees, may find themselves unable to stomach the idea of making unfair and financially painful payouts to unreasonable customers, no matter how rarely these customers present themselves.

Specific Guarantees

Fortunately, a guarantee doesn't have to unconditionally promise satisfaction to be extraordinary. Specific guarantees allow a company to spell out exactly which elements of the product or service it chooses to stand behind. If some other element fails, the company isn't obliged to compensate the customer, no matter how large his or her dissatisfaction.

While such a guarantee sounds—and often is—a great deal weaker than an unconditional guarantee of satisfaction, it need not be perceived as an inadequate guarantee by the customer. In fact, specific guarantees can be quite powerful. Furthermore, in addition to limiting or even eliminating unreasonable triggerings, a specific guarantee has the added advantage of focusing the customer's attention on that element of the product or service that the company would most like to stress, either because it is a high priority with the customer or because the company believes that it has a quality advantage in that area.

For manufacturers, the elements most often stressed are functionality and reliability. Thus standard product warranties don't promise that customers will enjoy the product for a long period of time, or even that the product will do everything the customer wants it to do; instead, they guarantee that the product won't malfunction or break. Because they are standard, such warranties rarely provide manufacturers with much marketing clout or quality improvement motivation. But there are ways of making product warranties stand out.

The simplest way to improve on a standard product guarantee is to extend its time limit. Electronic appliance manufacturer Curtis Mathes, for example, has managed to build a reputation as an extremely high-quality manufacturer—and to maintain an enviable profit margin—largely by including a six-year parts and labor warranty with its televisions and VCRs, compared to the industry standard one-year warranty. The auto industry, meanwhile, is a virtual battleground for warranty time extensions. Car warranties have crept up over the past decade from a standard one-year, 12,000-mile warranty to some that run as long as seven years. Largely for this reason, the cost to the automobile industry of honoring warranties jumped from $700 million in 1965 to $5 billion in 1988.[2] A lifetime guarantee for cars thus seems unlikely, but Ford has offered lifetime guarantees on its repairs: If something one of its dealers fixes needs rerepairing, the new repair is free. The industry has tried to manage warranty costs by experimenting with ways of limiting guarantees other than by time duration. Some companies provide longer warranties only on certain parts of the car, such as the power train, and GM even tried (unsuccessfully) to introduce a $100 deductible on warranty repairs.

A specific guarantee can help a manufacturer highlight or reinforce some of its product's strong points, and allows for focusing quality improvement and marketing efforts on those elements. Some carpeting manufacturers, for example, offer guarantees against staining or fading. And knowing that the world traveler image is one that appeals to its customers, Rolex offers guarantees on its watches that, unlike most product guarantees, allow for free servicing in major cities around the world.

Because it can be hard to measure the elements of a service, and because they often have to be delivered in adverse conditions (such as crowded restaurants, traffic-jammed streets, or rooms full of hostile executives), some service companies may have difficulty thinking up a practical specific guarantee. But many have done so to great benefit. One classic example is Domino's Pizza, which promised either to deliver a pizza within a half hour or provide the pizza for free. (Domino's has since modified the guarantee, as we will discuss later.) Federal Express is another example: Its guarantee to deliver packages by 10:30 A.M. of the next business day (to most locations) continues to inspire confidence on the part of its customers.

In fact, the ability of a specific guarantee to call attention to a product's strength is so beneficial that some companies willing to offer an unconditional guarantee of satisfaction may actually choose to disguise it as a specific guarantee. For example, the Trump Shuttle airline offered its customers an on-time arrival guarantee, noting with less emphasis that passengers could also trigger the guarantee if they were unsatisfied for any reason. Clearly, the unconditional guarantee of satisfaction made the on-time arrival guarantee redundant, but the company wanted to call special attention to its commitment to arriving on time. Likewise, Florsheim gave purchasers of its shoes thirty days to return the shoes for a refund if they found the shoes uncomfortable; but discomfort is so utterly subjective that the company was essentially offering an unconditional guarantee of satisfaction, phrased so as to stress the company's confidence in the comfortableness of its shoes.

Limiting the Scope of Guarantees

Some companies will find it too risky to offer even a specific guarantee that is extraordinary. Perhaps they don't yet have enough faith in their quality control systems—or in the honesty of their customers. Or perhaps their ability to provide customer satisfaction or to meet specific performance criteria is truly at the mercy of uncontrollable processes. For these companies, there are ways of limiting the risks of guarantees so that they can be extraordinary without being excessively dangerous or foolhardy. The obvious drawback to such risk reducers is that the less bold and potentially costly the payout is, the less impressed potential and actual customers will be and the less potential there is for improving the organization.

One way to tone down the risk of a guarantee is to require the customer to meet certain conditions that take some of the burden off the company. Such requirements make it possible to strongly guarantee products or services that would not normally lend themselves to such assurances. The pest elimination service PRISM, for example, is famous for its specific guarantee to completely eliminate cockroaches from restaurants, hotels, and other businesses. Before PRISM, such a guarantee was unthinkable; no matter how thoroughly an exterminator goes after cockroaches, they almost always re-emerge sooner or later. But PRISM was promising to get rid of them for good. The catch: Customers had to religiously follow the rigorous maintenance routines PRISM laid out for them. If the customer strayed from the routines, the guarantee was void. In fact, in these circumstances, PRISM would dump the customer altogether.

Lincoln Electric Company guaranteed its customers that it could reduce their welding costs by an amount determined ahead of time, and would pay the customer the difference between the promised amount and the actual savings, if the latter fell short. The catch: Customers had to let Lincoln scrutinize their welding practices and equipment and to follow any recommendations the company made.

Some tire companies have offered guarantees that span the life of the car—but only if the customer regularly brings the car in to the tire dealer for maintenance such as tire rotation. Some car rustproofing services have provided a similar guarantee. And pharmaceutical manufacturer G. D. Searle promised customers that they could get a full refund on their prescription medicines if they could produce a doctor's note saying that the medication was ineffective. Clearly, such requirements can cut down on the number of frivolous or unavoidable payouts; but if the requirements are too stringent or numerous, they will make the guarantee less than extraordinary.

Another way to lower the risk of extraordinary guarantees is to limit the payout for each triggering. By far the most common payout—and the one dissatisfied customers typically look for—is a full money-back refund. But customers of some companies, particularly of service companies with complex or spread-out fee structures, will feel that a guarantee offering partial payment is satisfactory, especially if the company is guaranteeing an element of its service for which customers don't normally expect high performance. Thus a number of banks have instituted a policy of guaranteeing such service elements as error-free checking, teller line waits of less than five minutes, or problem resolution in less than twenty-four hours; in each case, triggering the guarantee earns the customer a flat payment, usually five dollars (see Figure 4-2). The First National Bank of Chicago has offered a $250 payment to customers who are dissatisfied with their loan application process. Allied Van Lines, meanwhile, guaranteed that it

Figure 4-2. Minneapolis-based Marquette Banks' guarantee compensates customers for the smallest of errors.

If We're Off This Much,

We'll Pay You This Much.

If other financial institutions make a mistake with your checking account, all you're likely to get is an apology.

But, if we make a mistake with your checking account, we'll give you $5.

Nobody else in town offers this Performance Guarantee. But, then, nobody else offers a checking account as good as Marquette's Performance Checking.

There's no minimum balance required. No monthly service charges. You even get a free cash card and six free cash card withdrawals a month.

The only thing that you have to pay for is check printing.

Performance Checking is available only at Marquette Banks.

Don't make the mistake of opening a checking account anywhere else.

Marquette Banks

The Best News In Banking.

Source: Marquette Banks.

would get its customers moved on schedule or pay $100 for each day of delay.

But lest companies become too enamored of the idea of offering customers less-than-your-money-back guarantees, they should be aware that a competitor could make them look bad with a full money-back guarantee—or even a *more*-than-your-money-back guarantee. Speedy Muffler King offered such a bold guarantee on its muffler repairs, promising customers that they would receive all their money back if not satisfied, plus an additional 10 percent. Kelvinator has backed its freezers with a conventional warranty plus a promise of up to $250 to cover any food spoiled in a failure. And Quaker State Oil guarantees not merely the cost of a can of oil if it fails to lubricate engine parts adequately, but the cost of ruined engine parts for 250,000 miles or ten years. Whether or not the extra money would make up for lost time, aggravation, and incidental expenses, many customers will appreciate the gesture and assume that if the company is willing to risk losing money on each of its sales it must be especially sure of itself.

Another way of holding down guarantee risks is to offer to replace a product or service with the same type the customer had rather than to refund the money. The cost of a replacement-only payout is usually far less to the company than a refund, and prevents the customer from taking the money and running to a competitor. In essence, it forces the customer to give the company a second chance to prove its worth. Scruba-dub Car Wash, for example, promises customers it will wash their cars again and again until they're satisfied the car is clean. Whirlpool provides an unconditional one-year replacement guarantee on its appliances. Xerox does the same for its copier customers for three years. And Mannington Resilient Floors' top-of-the-line vinyl flooring comes with a one-year replacement unconditional guarantee.

A possible disadvantage of a replacement-only guarantee is that some customers will mistrust the idea of being forced to accept the same product after having had a bad experience with it, and thus will not regard the guarantee as a powerful one. In addition, once again, competitors can turn the tables with a stronger version, for instance, a replacement-with-a-competitor guarantee, in which the company offers to replace an unsatisfactory product or service with a competitor's product or service. PRISM, the pest eliminator, for example, offers to pay a competitor's fee for one year if PRISM fails to rid a customer of cockroaches. Canadian supermarket chain Loblaws, meanwhile, offered to replace its private-label food items with national brands if customers didn't consider Loblaws's a better value. (Such bravery doesn't always require sacrifice: Only 1,500 out of 15 million items were returned to Loblaws under the guarantee.)

Even less risky than a replacement-only guarantee is a repair-only guarantee. Although a promise to repair is part of standard product warranties, such guarantees can be made extraordinary by making the process more convenient. Steward Wattley Cranes, for example, guarantees its customers that it will repair cranes within twenty-four hours. And Jaguar provides a free loaner Jaguar to any Jaguar owner who needs to have his or her car repaired under warranty.

Some service companies offer a no-fee-until guarantee, in which customers are told that they won't be billed until some performance requirement is met. At first glance, such a guarantee might seem even riskier than a standard full money-back guarantee; after all, with the latter a company at least has the customer's money in hand to start with. But, in fact, the no-fee-until version offers some extra protection to the offerer: If customers are dissatisfied, they can't simply ask for their money back and flee; instead, they will probably give the company additional time to make good on its promised level of service. Could manufacturers offer a no-payment-until guarantee? Some car dealerships have taken a step in this direction, allowing customers to take "extended test drives" that last up to three days. It would be a huge leap, however, to allow customers to keep the car until they feel satisfied enough to pay for it.

Unusual Types of Payouts

Companies that face a unique challenge in offering guarantees, or that otherwise want to make their guarantees stand out without taking wild risks, can try to be creative about the sorts of payouts they offer.

How does a company guarantee its service, for example, if a customer is supposed to *make* money on the service, as in a money market fund? One way is to guarantee the amount of money a customer will make, promising to pay the difference between the promised amount and the actual earnings. Sotheby's art auction house offers such a guarantee to some of its clients; if an individual item or a particular lot of items brings in less than the company said it would, Sotheby's makes up the shortfall. And as mentioned earlier, Lincoln Electric paid customers the difference between their actual welding cost savings and the savings Lincoln promised they would achieve if they followed its recommendations.

Some companies try to add a personal touch to their guarantees by staying away from straight financial compensation. Insurance company Empire of America, for example, buys lunch for customers who have to wait in line more than five minutes. First Union National Bank of Charlotte, North Carolina, has managers deliver a dozen roses to customers victimized by bank errors. The University of Alabama at Birmingham provides free car wash coupons to students who have to wait more than ten minutes for a response from the school's security department (small compensation if they are experiencing a violent crime, but not bad if they simply need a jump start for their car). Electronic component supplier Pioneer offered to buy its customers a collector's model pink Cadillac if it failed to ship a certain type of component on time.

Some organizations recognize that their business customers' highest priority is to satisfy their own customers. These companies can offer pass-through guarantees, in which the customers' customers are the immediate beneficiary. PRISM tells its restaurant and hotel customers that it will pay for the meal or room, respectively, of any patron who spots a cockroach, and will also pay for a second complimentary meal or room at a later time; it also sends patrons a letter of apology. Monsanto Company guarantees that the fibers it sells to customers will perform as promised in the clothing, carpeting, and upholstery its customers manufacture; Monsanto's customers can then pass this guarantee on to their customers. In an unusual twist on this idea, the Los Angeles public school system guarantees its students that employers will find them sufficiently educated; otherwise, the employer can send the hiree back to school for extra classes.

Faced with such a wide variety of possible payouts, some companies might despair over selecting the one most appropriate for them. Actually, they don't have to choose; they can leave it up to the customer. Many product warranties allow customers to pick repair, replacement, or refund. A number of consulting firms give customers the option of getting their money back, getting part of their money back to reflect their degree of dissatisfaction (a sliding-scale guarantee), or letting the firm work for free until the customer is satisfied. The Trump Shuttle gave its late or otherwise dissatisfied passengers a choice of 2,000 frequent flyer miles, a half-price companion ticket, or a $20 discount good at a number of top-notch restaurants.

Perhaps the only payout more effective than one the customer picks is one that provides the customer with *all* the types of payouts simultaneously. PRISM offers just such a tour-de-force guarantee: If cockroaches reappear while the service is in force, the company refunds one year's worth of fees, offers the pass-through guarantee mentioned earlier, and pays for up to a year's worth of a competitor's services; in addition, if the problem results in a health department violation, PRISM pays any fines and gives its customer $5,000 if it is temporarily shut down.

At the opposite extreme from the tour-de-force guarantee is the meaningless guarantee—a guarantee that doesn't pay out anything. Warranty law prevents such bogus guarantees on products, but services can avail themselves of this dubious tactic. The owners of the Pittsburgh Pirates baseball team offered fans just such a useless entity: They "guaranteed" that the team would make the playoffs. There was no offer of free tickets if the team failed, no nothing, in fact—just disappointed fans.

Implicit Guarantees

But that doesn't mean that a company has to specify a payout, or any other element of the guarantee, to make customers feel more than adequately protected. Many companies operate successfully with an implicit guarantee—a guarantee that isn't expressly stated but that customers feel they can count on anyway. As mentioned before, Nordstrom department stores are well-known for their willingness to compensate dissatisfied customers; legend has it that they once provided refunds for tires—even though the stores don't sell tires. (Wisely, the company will not publicly confirm or deny this story.) Yet nowhere in its stores or promotional materials does Nordstrom specifically say that it offers any sort of guarantee.

Fine restaurants and hotels offer implicit guarantees. So do some inexpensive ones: Customers complaining about food are generally whisked replacements or refunds, despite the lack of any promise that the company would do so. (Interestingly, McDonald's chose in 1992 to make its guarantee explicit.)

Companies that inspire their customers to feel that an implicit guarantee of satisfaction is in place are in an enviable position. For one thing, they do not have to worry about making unreasonably large or frequent payouts, because they haven't specified what the company will do in the event of a product or service failure. (Of course, manufacturers must at a minimum provide the remedies mandated by warranty law; but an implicit guarantee can allow them to go well above and beyond.) Companies can thus tailor the self-punishment to fit the crime, helping a consulting firm, for example, to avoid the risk of having to pay out $50,000 because it served stale muffins at a coffee break. On the other hand, a company can choose to shower a customer with a payout that is far more generous than any the client might have asked for, creating feelings of profound satisfaction.

Companies offering an implicit guarantee also don't have to worry about a guarantee appearing unseemly or as just another form of marketing hype. Instead, they can be perceived by customers as simply wanting to do what's right. For example, a small company called Flyaway Avian Averting Systems, which prevents birds from roosting on its customers' buildings, doesn't send out a bill until the customer reports that the birds are gone for good. The company doesn't apprise customers of this policy ahead of time; it simply depends on customers telling other, potential customers about their satisfaction. And Child Development Products, a toy company that sells by catalog, authorizes its hotline operators to provide refunds of up to $25 over the phone, although it never brags of its generous refund policies. Professional and other upscale service firms in particular prefer to avoid the possible marketing backlash that an explicit guarantee risks. Although their customers may infer essentially the same protection, not having to state it explicitly avoids raising suspicions of potential nonperformance and creating the appearance of enlisting tacky marketing techniques. An implicit guarantee is generally perceived as a classier way to impart an image of reliability.

Unfortunately, implicit guarantees can't simply be thrown into place. They have to be earned through instance after instance of making good on customer dissatisfaction. The implicit guarantee then has to wend its way into customers' consciousness; after all, if the company simply announced that it offered an implicit guarantee, the guarantee wouldn't be implicit anymore. Implicit guarantees can be implied in marketing efforts, but the message is unlikely to be effective unless it is backed up by a solid reputation for high-quality work and for applying the guarantee when the customer is not satisfied. Start-up companies or firms with an unimpressive performance history can commit themselves to an implicit guarantee, but will probably not win many clients with it. Thus the offering of an implicit guarantee might best be viewed as part of a later stage in a firm's quality evolution, a stage that is perhaps best preceded by positive experiences with an explicit unconditional guarantee.

A company can also ease itself into an implicit guarantee by offering an explicit guarantee that covers a portion of its product or service offerings and employing an implicit guarantee to cover the remainder. The implicit guarantee then acts as a safety net, catching dissatisfied customers before they leave the system and compensating them to restore their satisfaction. Because customers may not be aware of the implicit guarantee—and may therefore not bring problems to the firm's attention—frontline employees need to be especially vigilant to detect errors and instances of customer dissatisfaction.

Having an implicit guarantee doesn't mean that a company shouldn't be proactive about letting customers know that they are entitled to compensation. Ford made this mistake when it discovered that the paint on some of its trucks was cracking and fading prematurely. Admirably, Ford covered the problem as if it had an implicit guarantee in effect, repainting trucks even if the warranty had lapsed. Less admirably, Ford provided this coverage only to customers who caught the defect; apparently the company had no intention of notifying other customers of the problem. When the defect and Ford's policy were written about in the press, customers and consumer protection agencies howled. True, the minority of customers who had their trucks repainted felt that Ford had acted generously; but, on the whole, the affair was something of a public relations and customer satisfaction debacle.

In general, companies should take great care in choosing the type of extraordinary guarantee that is most suitable to their needs. As we'll see in the next chapter, this process can be a complex one; but if carried out properly, it will result in a guarantee that is far more likely to help than to hurt.

Notes

1. "Counselor to the King," *New York Times* (Sept. 24, 1989), Sec. 6, Part 2, p. 18.
2. Melvyn A. J. Menezes, "Leverage Your Warranty Program," *Sloan Management Review* (Summer 1990), p. 69.

Chapter 5

Designing the Guarantee

In 1987, Xerox executives learned from a survey that customers didn't believe that the company had made customer satisfaction a top concern. These findings were disturbing to managers, who had decreed that customer satisfaction was to be one of the company's prime goals. Furthermore, under the belief that product quality was the single most important element of customer satisfaction, Xerox was well along on a five-year quality improvement program that ultimately won the company a Baldrige Award, the prestigious award presented each year by the U.S. Department of Commerce to the highest-quality American companies.

The president of Xerox decided that the company needed some way to better align the image it was projecting to customers with the internal goals it had set for itself. His decision: The company would offer an extraordinary guarantee. To design it, he pulled together a team of managers and employees representing almost every function in the company. The team soon recommended a ninety-day, unconditional money-back guarantee, unmatched in the office equipment industry.

Xerox shared the idea with a number of customers to get their reaction. To management's surprise, they didn't like it. Ninety days wasn't long enough, most said; a copy machine or other sophisticated piece of equipment should work perfectly for years, and a manufacturer should be willing to stand behind it for an extended period of time. In addition, customers weren't keen on money-back refunds. Asking for your money back on an office machine, many of them said, raises doubts among bosses and associates as to the wisdom of your initial decision to purchase the product. Rather than wanting protection against a bad decision, customers wanted protection against getting a particular unit that turned out to be a lemon.

The Xerox guarantee team went back to the drawing board and came up with a second version, also unmatched in the industry: a three-year unconditional replacement guarantee. If, for any reason, a customer wasn't completely satisfied with a Xerox product, the product could be returned and replaced with an identical or equivalent unit. Customers approved, and the guarantee was put into effect in September of 1990. That guarantee remains a cornerstone of Xerox's marketing and quality programs (see Figure 5-1).

Xerox's efforts to design a guarantee incorporated several elements often overlooked by companies seeking to introduce an extraordinary guarantee:

- Xerox solicited and examined customers' perceptions of the company and its guarantee.
- The company took into account its ability to produce quality products and services.
- It chose a guarantee whose scope and compensation went beyond industry standards.
- It made sure that the guarantee directly addressed key customer concerns.
- The company kept the guarantee simple and easy to invoke.
- It aligned the guarantee with company priorities.

The success Xerox has enjoyed with its guarantee program is largely attributable to the care it took in ensuring that it selected the right guarantee for the right reasons. By the same token, many guarantee programs have failed because elements of the guarantee design process were ignored. This chapter lists the questions a company should ask itself before embarking on a guarantee program in order to ensure both that the guarantee is effective and that it addresses the company's specific needs and situation.

Figure 5-1.   Xerox's guarantee focuses the entire organization on ensuring full customer satisfaction.

Finally, a guarantee that lets you decide if you're satisfied.

Introducing the Xerox Total Satisfaction Guarantee
Some guarantees guarantee products. Some guarantee service. And some have so much fine print, the only thing you're guaranteed is confusion. But the Xerox Total Satisfaction Guarantee is so simple, you'll think it's too good to be true. It says, if you're not satisfied with your Xerox equipment, we'll replace it. And only you tell us when you're satisfied.

What follows is the entire guarantee in all its simplicity. But don't read it as a guarantee, read it as a reflection of the confidence we have in our quality equipment, dedicated support and service.

"If you are not satisfied with your Xerox equipment, at your request, Xerox will replace it without charge to you with an identical model or a machine with comparable features and capabilities.

"The term of the Xerox Total Satisfaction Guarantee is three years from equipment delivery. If the newly delivered

equipment is financed by Xerox for more than 3 years, the Guarantee will apply during the entire term of your Xerox financing.

"This Xerox Total Satisfaction Guarantee applies to Xerox equipment acquired by you from Xerox—including Sales Agents and participating Dealers and Retailers—and continuously maintained by Xerox or its authorized representatives under our Manufacturer's Warranty or a Service Contract. This guarantee applies to all equipment acquired on or after September 5, 1990."

If you'd like more information about this unprecedented guarantee and our quality products, call us at 1-800-TEAM-XRX, ext. 908B.

XEROX
The Document Company

© 1990 XEROX Corporation. XEROX® is a trademark of XEROX Corporation.

Source: Courtesy of Xerox Corporation.

Deciding Who Decides

The first step in the guarantee design process is to build enthusiasm for the concept and then to establish the decision-making and evaluation framework in which the process will take place. The key questions to ask are:

■ *Is there a guarantee champion in the company?* Guarantee programs rarely get off the ground unless there is at least one influential person in the company who believes strongly in the idea of an extraordinary guarantee, who can generate support for the idea, and who will maintain enthusiasm for the project during those inevitable rocky periods when other people's commitment temporarily wavers.

■ *Is senior management committed to a guarantee?* If the champion is a senior manager, as was the case with Xerox, the process can proceed. Otherwise, the champion will have to continue his or her efforts until top management has bought into the concept. Proceeding with a guarantee program when there is only a half-hearted commitment from senior management is usually a mistake; no matter how well-thought-out the guarantee design may be, unenthusiastic executives will probably balk when it comes time to provide the resources necessary to implement the guarantee.

■ *Is the guarantee design a team effort?* When senior managers are convinced of the potential of a guarantee, their best initial move is to set up a team to take responsibility for studying the pros and cons of a guarantee, and to recommend the form a guarantee should take. The larger and more cross-functional the team is, the better it will be; not only does this breadth provide more perspective on all the issues that will be raised by a strong guarantee, it also ensures greater buy-in throughout the organization if and when the guarantee program is implemented.

Larger organizations may require a multilevel approach. The high-level team appointed by senior management can set up a task force to come up with a detailed design for a guarantee, leaving for itself the job of setting the task force's direction and reviewing its recommendations. The task force might then set up breakout groups to examine particular aspects of the project, such as quality, cost/benefits, and competitive assessment.

• *Are customers providing input?* Regardless of how the guarantee design project is structured, feedback from customers at every step of the way is crucial. Companies should repeatedly invite key customers, either singly or in a group, to meet with the guarantee design team; they should also make use of focus groups and surveys.

When the decision-making channels are established and customer input has been made available, the company will be ready to confront the key decisions in the guarantee design process: whether or not to offer a guarantee; whether to make the guarantee explicit or implicit; whether to make the guarantee unconditional or specific; what to guarantee; what to offer as a payout; and what restrictions, if any, to place on the guarantee.

When a Guarantee Makes Sense—and When It Doesn't

The decision to offer a guarantee represents a major commitment, philosophically and operationally, and should be made only after assessing every aspect of the organization, its industry, and its market. Along the way, a company may decide that an extraordinary guarantee is inappropriate. Here are the questions to be considered:

• *How high are quality standards?* Some companies will recognize that quality standards are already high for themselves and their industries, and are perceived to be such by customers. In this case, a company may not get much marketing or operational mileage from issuing a guarantee. To advertise or promote the obvious would produce few benefits, and might actually be perceived as incongruent with a company's high-quality image. A guarantee is also unlikely to positively differentiate a company in an industry or industry segment where operating standards are uniformly high and customers routinely expect excellent products or service. By the same token, commodity companies that compete almost solely on the basis of price may fail to gain any ground with customers through a guarantee, unless it is a price guarantee.

- *How high is customer risk?* All other things being equal, the need for a guarantee is roughly proportional to the level of perceived risk a customer faces in doing business with an organization. Perceived risk is usually higher with companies offering unproven, unfamiliar, and complex products (say, a high-speed computer network, as opposed to a toaster), or with those offering highly intangible services, as do many consulting firms. Some industries, historically, have never achieved high levels of trust among customers; the used car business is an example. An unusually powerful guarantee could be a lifesaver to such companies. On the other hand, companies offering straightforward products or services familiar to and trusted by customers may not have as much to gain from a guarantee.

- *Are competitors offering a guarantee?* Obviously, competitors' positions regarding guarantees should have a big influence on a company's decision to offer a guarantee. If one or more competitors have enhanced their success through strong guarantees, a company would be wise to follow their lead. If competitors don't offer exceptional guarantees, offering a guarantee may not be a necessity; it may, however, represent an opportunity to obtain a competitive edge by being a first mover and establishing quality leadership—an edge that might be hard to blunt. In any case, a company that ignores guarantees under the assumption that its competitors will do the same risks being taken by surprise when a competitor does introduce a guarantee. Companies will be far better off approaching this difficult terrain proactively, at their own pace, than they will be if forced to rush ahead to catch up to a rival.

- *Is a guarantee compatible with company culture?* Companies that have already dedicated themselves to customer satisfaction and high quality will usually not find the transition to formal guarantees a difficult one. On the other hand, organizations that have kept these goals in the background, behind market share or profitability, may find that their entire culture is resistant to making the profound changes necessary to support an extraordinary guarantee. Thus McDonald's longtime emphasis on "QSCV"—quality, service, cleanliness, and value—has prepared that company well for a guarantee; the U.S. Post Office, on the other hand, with its constant emphasis on cost reduction and efficiency, would have to struggle to survive a broad, powerful guarantee.

- *Can you afford a guarantee?* There are two costs associated with a guarantee program: the cost of guarantee payouts and the cost of raising quality so as to reduce payouts. (One could also consider the marketing costs associated with communicating the guarantee to customers; but these costs aren't necessarily incremental, in that the required marketing efforts can piggyback on or take the place of other marketing programs.) Theoretically, a company could virtually eliminate payout costs by raising quality to the point where there were almost no flaws, but the cost of doing so would be prohibitive for most companies. Likewise, a company could ignore quality and simply make whatever payouts resulted; but if the guarantee is truly extraordinary, the resulting payout costs will also be "extraordinary."

A more practical course is to minimize the sum of the payout and quality costs by raising quality to the point where the cost of adding more quality would substantially outweigh the payouts. But even if a company could identify and achieve this optimal quality point—often a difficult task in itself—the resulting costs may still be too high. Ultimately, of course, the increased revenues and profits that come from providing higher quality and a strong guarantee could and should overtake these costs, but some companies can't survive the wait.

Predicting the cost of payouts is difficult at best. Traditionally, manufacturers budget anywhere from one percent to 25 percent of sales to cover warranty costs. But however much a company is used to paying out on an ordinary guarantee (and most service companies aren't used to paying out *anything*), that figure may prove irrelevant to the payout rate of an extraordinary guarantee. A company can anticipate payouts swelling at first from the broader coverage and larger payout of an extraordinary guarantee, and then shrinking as the company gets a handle on the quality flaws exposed by the guarantee. But beyond this rough estimation, it would be unwise to put much confidence in a guess as to where the payout rate will hover at any particular time.

Although companies can come up with a solid estimate for the cost of a traditional quality-raising program, these figures may again prove irrelevant to the company that is forced to raise quality under the gun of a guarantee program; the costs could be higher or lower than expected (fortunately, as we shall see later, most companies find them to be lower). Perhaps a better way to look at the question is this: Can you afford *not* to raise quality, guarantee or no guarantee? Given the sea change in consumer values over the past decade, it is fair to say that in some industries those companies that can't raise quality significantly will be run out of business by quality-savvy competitors in the United States and abroad. Companies in these industries can't worry about whether or not they can afford to raise quality; they must simply try to find the best way to do it.

Unfortunately, many companies will recognize that they just don't have the resources to quickly lift quality even to industry standards. One survey of travel agencies, for example, found that while the industry norm for errors (failing to find the least expensive fare, for example) was 2 to 5 percent, some agencies had error rates of 40 percent. It is likely that some of these agencies have systems and cultures so riddled with inefficiencies and ineptitude that a raise-quality-fast-or-die program would result in death. These companies will want to stay away from guarantees. Ironically, the companies that are in the best position to offer extraordinary guarantees—those with superb quality and recognized as such by customers—are generally not in dire need of the benefits they promise (though the benefits would of course be welcome). Guarantees are ideal, on the other hand, for those companies that need to lift quality and make an impression on customers, but that aren't in the depths of poor-quality perdition.

Companies that decide to bail out of the guarantee design process at this point haven't suffered a total loss. Even though the organization may have determined that an extraordinary guarantee and its attendant risks are too intimidating, it may also have discovered that the experience of merely considering implementing a guarantee was enough to shake up the organization and to inspire it to address its quality shortcomings.

Choosing Between Explicit and Implicit Guarantees

If a company has decided that it is a candidate for an extraordinary guarantee, it should first determine whether it will be better off committing itself to an explicit or an implicit guarantee. For the most part, only service companies need go through this exercise, because manufacturers must by law offer explicit guarantees, even if it is only the minimal explicit guarantee provided by state law. (Although these legally mandated minimal warranties are termed "implied" warranties, they are explicit in the sense that they are spelled out in the Uniform Commercial Code.) Of course, a manufacturer could add a strong implicit guarantee to supplement a less-powerful explicit one; but it's hard to see how such a policy would benefit the company, since customers would almost certainly assume that the lesser, explicit warranty was the one that took priority. For example, while most car companies occasionally make free repairs after a warranty has expired, these generosities have done little to convince buyers that the companies are eager to go beyond their explicit warranties. Thus the following questions apply primarily to service companies:

- *What is the company's track record on customer satisfaction?* A company probably shouldn't consider an implicit guarantee if it does not have a well-established history of bending over backward to satisfy customers. The implicit guarantee offered by the Four Seasons hotel chain builds on that organization's reputation for above-and-beyond hospitality and fanatic error recovery; for example, those rare guests who are "bumped"—that is, whose reserved rooms are not available—are not surprised to find that the unstated policy of the hotel is to whisk them by luxury limousine to the nearest first-class hotel for free accommodations. The Marriott hotels, on the other hand, opted for a set of explicit guarantees that, among other things, promises guests who are bumped a cash payment of $200 in addition to transportation to a free room at another hotel.

- *How costly will it be to communicate the guarantee?* A business that has many relatively painless opportunities to prove its commitment to customer satisfaction has a better chance of successfully implementing an implicit guarantee than one that has to suffer through occasional but traumatic payouts. Thus restaurants can easily communicate an implicit guarantee by enthusiastically "comping" meals for inconvenienced customers; a wedding caterer, on the other hand, might end up waiving a substantial portion of its yearly income before a significant percentage of its customers got the word that this firm will do whatever it takes to satisfy its clientele.

- *Can you afford to wait for the benefits?* Start-ups or companies facing severe competitive threats may be in dire need of the immediate marketing boost that an explicit guarantee can provide. Only organizations willing and able to make a long-term investment in customer satisfaction and quality would do well to consider implicit guarantees; the payoff from that investment can be considerable, but it may also be a long time in coming, and many companies are not in a position to wait.

Weighing the Unconditional Guarantee

An unconditional guarantee can provide substantially greater marketing and quality benefits than other types of explicit guarantees. But telling customers that they can demand a payout for any reason whatsoever exposes a company to considerable risk if it can't precisely identify all customer needs and expectations, as well as all elements, controllable and uncontrollable, that could lead to these needs and expectations not being met. In other words, a company shouldn't attempt to guarantee total satisfaction unless it understands all the factors that affect satisfaction. The following questions can help determine whether or not a company is ready for an unconditional guarantee:

- *Will an unconditional guarantee cost a manufacturer much more than a conventional warranty?* For most manufacturing companies, customer satisfaction is hugely dependent on product functionality and reliability. These qualities are relatively easy to measure. If the product does what it is supposed to do, and doesn't break, most customers are satisfied and will not invoke the guarantee. These two elements, of course, are guaranteed in standard product warranties. The benefit to a customer of an unconditional product guarantee, then, lies in the customer's ability to return the product in those rarer instances when he or she is dissatisfied with a product that is functioning properly and reliably. A customer might, for example, be tempted to return a product because the instruction manual was confusing, a competitor introduced a better-performing product, the product became dirty or scratched, or the color lost its appeal.

Traditionally, these are not acceptable grounds for returning a product to a manufacturer, and some of them are unreasonable. But what percentage of a customer base will invoke a guarantee on entirely unreasonable grounds? And how does that additional cost compare with the marketing boost and increased customer loyalty that such a powerful guarantee can provide?

Xerox and General Electric, two of the most admired companies in the world, have both decided that the message their unconditional guarantees send to customers earns them far more in customer loyalty than it costs them in additional payouts. It is inevitable that other manufacturers will follow suit. Low-quality manufacturers should stay away from unconditional guarantees, however. Even though they already bear the costs of servicing outright defective products, the additional cost of paying out to customers irritated by minor flaws and overall shabbiness could be overwhelming.

- *Is your service measurable?* Service companies may have an additional motivation for going with an unconditional guarantee rather than a specific guarantee: It is often difficult to measure the elements of customer satisfaction. What is "courteous" service? What is "useful" financial advice? What is a "comfortable" room? Ultimately, customers must pass judgment on such parameters using their own entirely subjective standards. Such vague concepts cannot often be meaningfully delineated for the purposes of a specific guarantee, and thus many service providers find that the *only* way they can powerfully guarantee their offerings is with an unconditional guarantee of satisfaction. (Manufacturers of consumables, such as canned food products, cosmetics, and pharmaceuticals, are often in the same boat; many of these companies, such as Procter & Gamble, do in fact offer unconditional guarantees with their products.)

- *What are the uncontrollables?* Some companies are subject to too many uncontrollable elements to permit them to safely consider an unconditional guarantee. Airlines and medical facilities, for example, are typically in this situation. But companies in such businesses can sometimes pull off an unconditional guarantee by restricting it to certain, more predictable services. As mentioned earlier, the Trump Shuttle offered a successful unconditional guarantee, largely because many of the vagaries of air travel are minimized on the short, well-serviced runs to which the Shuttle was restricted. And the Henry Ford Hospital in Detroit decided that its diagnostic radiology department could offer an unconditional guarantee after it had surveyed customers and discovered that most cases of dissatisfaction resulted from patients having to wait too long or from encounters with rude or indifferent employees. Thus by focusing its quality efforts on eliminating waits and training employees to be more courteous, the department greatly reduced the risk of payouts from the guarantee.

- *Is the company particularly susceptible to unreasonable triggerings?* Any company offering an unconditional guarantee must live with the problem of unreasonable triggerings. Organizations that have a history of antagonizing customers will be particularly subject to such triggerings, even if the company has completely cleaned up its act. Thus Continental Airlines, despite having partially recovered from the deterioration of service it experienced when the company first fell on hard times in the 1980s, would be at risk for excessive triggerings by the large number of travelers who would like to exact revenge for the shabby treatment they received in the past. Such companies would be wise to put more time between themselves and their transgressions before offering an unconditional guarantee.

Unreasonable triggerings can be particularly painful for professional service firms, which often work long and hard to satisfy a small number of clients. But even for these firms, the gain may be worth the pain. One consultant offering an unconditional guarantee, for example, was told by a client that he should have provided a full, formal report at the end of a project—despite the fact that the client had initially agreed to a summary report to hold down costs. The consultant responded by providing a full report at no extra cost. Another client told the same consultant that he was surprised to receive a bill for services that he believed should have been considered part of the consultant's marketing efforts—apparently having forgotten that the consultant had specifically discussed with him the point at which billing would commence. The consultant waived the fee without argument.

How does the consultant feel about unconditional guarantees after two unreasonable triggerings? Completely enthusiastic: The first client has gone on to engage the consultant on several larger projects, and the second client has proved to be a valuable reference and promises to sign on soon for a significant piece of business. Not all firms, however, would be able to take such a long view of the situation.

Defining the Specific Guarantee

Companies that prefer the more manageable risks of a specific guarantee to the uncertainties of an unconditional guarantee must decide what it is, exactly, that they are going to guarantee. In some cases this is a complex question, and answering it can require a great deal of research and more than a little creativity. These questions can serve as a guide:

- *What is important to customers?* The most obvious elements to guarantee are the ones about which customers care the most. For products, quality and functionality are usually key elements; that's why manufacturers' standard warranties explicitly address them. But some manufacturers can gain an advantage from guaranteeing not only that the product will work, but that it will work *well*. Copy machine manufacturer Lanier, for example, though shying away from matching Xerox's unconditional replacement guarantee, determined through customer research that a key customer concern is that a copier will spend too much time out of commission due to servicing requirements. Thus Lanier now guarantees its copiers' "uptime"—that is, the percentage of time that the copier is working. Likewise, some window manufacturers that boast of their products' thermal insulation properties guarantee that customers' fuel bills will be reduced by a certain percentage, or the manufacturer pays the difference.

Service companies can employ customer research to identify one or two key elements of customer satisfaction out of the complex tangle of elements that often characterize these businesses. Avis, for example, found that the thing its rental car customers fear above all else is not long lines, a lack of available cars, or overcharging, but mechanical breakdowns on the road. Thus Avis intends to incorporate breakdown protection into a planned guarantee. Brunswick Recreation Centers discovered that patrons of its bowling alleys worried that clumsy ball-return machines might chip or crack their personal bowling balls, and that jammed pin-setting equipment would interrupt games. Therefore, the company promised to replace damaged balls and to waive the cost of interrupted games. Vacationers tremble at the thought of lousy weather, but there isn't much anyone can do about that. Or is there? Holiday Inn of the Cayman Islands guarantees its scuba diving customers that if the weather isn't nice, the excursion is free.

- *What is the company good at?* In addition to seeking out customers' hot buttons, companies should also consider which of its capabilities are particularly strong. Even guaranteeing something that is only of secondary concern to customers can have impact if the company's capabilities allow it to promise exceptional performance. The Wells Fargo Bank determined that only one out of a thousand customers had to wait in line more than five minutes before it promised five dollars to any customer who wasn't helped within five minutes. Allied Van Lines' no-delay guarantee grew out of the company's confidence in a new computerized shipment tracking system. And although Delta Hotels wasn't prepared to match the broad guarantees of some of its rivals, it had beefed up its front-desk coverage to the point where it could guarantee its customers a one-minute check-in or a free room.

- *Are there service or product elements that need emphasizing?* Companies interested in calling attention to some aspect of their offerings that customers might otherwise overlook can do so with a specific guarantee. Although such guarantees are often less meaningful than those addressing key customer concerns, they can function as effective marketing tools. One ski resort eager to tap into the family market offered a kids-have-fun-or-it's-free guarantee. Although essentially unconditional (how could the resort challenge a customer's claim that a child didn't have fun?), the guarantee served to plant in potential customers' minds the idea that the resort was a great place to bring kids.

Along the same lines, GE offered a ten-year guarantee on the durability of a new extrarugged material it incorporated into its dishwashers, emphasizing both the presence and benefits of the new substance. And Olympus pushed the notion that its cameras allow the average consumer to take better pictures by offering customers one dollar for every bad picture they took. These guarantees work because they promise customers something unexpected. A guarantee that merely upholds the status quo, by contrast, will accomplish little. For example, it's hard to see how travelers could be impressed by Pan Am's guarantee that its first-class customers would receive excellent service.

- *Is the service a well-defined one?* Unlike manufacturers or companies such as restaurants or package couriers that offer well-defined services, some firms provide services whose elements are somewhat blurry in the minds of potential customers. It might seem as if such a company would have a hard time coming up with a specific guarantee, but, in fact, a specific guarantee can help define the service. Donnelly Directory, a company that publishes yellow-pages directories, promises advertisers that it will (among other things) provide a proof of the ad fifteen days before the sales close date and that customers can make changes in the ad up to the sales close date. For customers who know little about the process of placing an ad, this guarantee helps make some of the steps more tangible and sets clearer expectations—namely, that customers will have plenty of time to look over and modify the ad they'll be running. In test marketing, Donnelly found that this guarantee inspired more customer confidence than a guarantee that stated, "Absolute customer satisfaction, period."

Colleges offer another example of a vaguely defined service. When students "purchase" education, what are they actually buying? A degree? Knowledge? Wisdom? Job skills? Employability? A guarantee that promised simply to provide "a good education" would probably do little to reassure students or the parents paying for the education or employers hiring graduates of the school. Henry Ford Community College addresses this problem with a guarantee to refund the tuition for any course passed at the school for which another college doesn't grant credit, and to provide free courses to graduates whose employers find them lacking in the skills normally expected of a graduate. This guarantee highlights concrete benefits of the school's services and assures potential students that they will achieve these benefits.

Even some professional service firms, whose results can be nearly impossible to assess accurately, can come up with clearly measurable parameters on which to focus a guarantee. These might include meeting deadlines, helping customers to achieve a certain level of profitability, or allocating a specified number of staff people to a customer. Such quantified guarantees create clear expectations for a business that might otherwise be perceived as foggy. One management consulting firm specializing in just-in-time process management, for example, guarantees to reduce customers' setup time—the time it takes to modify a machine to make a different product—by at least 75 percent. Should the firm fail to meet that objective within the agreed-upon time frame, it works for free until the 75 percent threshold is reached. Reasonable men and women may disagree about a consultant's overall effectiveness, but they should not have as hard a time deciding how long it takes to set up a machine.

Even a firm that can't come up with discrete measurables might do well to offer a specific guarantee based on some nebulous but important element of service in order to assure customers that the firm is focusing on the appropriate goals. One management-strategy consulting firm offered the following specific guarantee: "We guarantee that at the completion of the project you will have the necessary and sufficient information to make the right decision about optimization of your process. If you don't, at your discretion, we will refund your money or work for free until you are satisfied." Although the vagueness of "necessary and sufficient information" renders this specific guarantee essentially unconditional, by pinpointing the nature of the desired output the guarantee probably has more impact than a straight unconditional guarantee of satisfaction would have.

Determining the Payout

For most companies, the most appropriate payout on a guarantee is a full refund. In general, guarantee terms that provide for less than a full refund should be employed with caution, because they can undermine the value of the guarantee. The point of a guarantee is to cover customers' costs when things go wrong, and limitations on the payout could raise questions about whether these costs will indeed be covered; they may also call into question the provider's confidence in not having to face a payout. In addition, a limited payout may not be stringent enough to force the organization to commit itself to taking every step possible to prevent errors from occurring. Still, there are exceptions to the suitability of a full refund, as the following questions illustrate:

- *Will a refund send the wrong message?* That was the case with Xerox's customers; the company found that people who purchase office equipment are loath to take the money and run because of the implication that the purchase was a mistake. In general, if customers are staking their reputation on a purchase decision and are heavily invested in it, they are probably more interested in a payout that focuses on making them happy with the product than in one that cuts them loose.

- *Is it clear what constitutes a full refund?* Some firms offer services for which many different types of fees are collected over an extended period of time; in this case, it is not always obvious what a "full refund" entails. A bank checking account customer, for example, pays monthly fees. But how many months' worth of fees should be returned to the customer in a program that guarantees satisfaction with the bank's service— and should the bank also consider refunding the interest it has earned on the customer's money? The question becomes even more complicated if the customer also has savings accounts and loans at the bank. That's why most banks offer a flat payout with their guarantee programs.

  If the difficulty lies solely with the fact that the service and associated fees are ongoing, the company can set a time limit on how far back it will go in refunding fees. Thus PRISM offers to refund a year's worth of fees to its dissatisfied customers. Professional service firms can often divide their services into fairly well-defined chunks, such as the phases of a consulting contract or the various steps in an architectural design project. These firms can then offer guarantees that promise to refund fees associated with one or more of the individual chunks. This approach limits the loss involved in a single triggering, and may also give the firm an opportunity to part ways with the client if additional misfortunes seem inevitable—though it would obviously be preferable to try to turn things around in the next phase.

- *Could a full refund make customers feel guilty?* A guarantee program is almost useless if customers don't feel comfortable invoking it. That can happen if a company offers a full refund even in situations where customer dissatisfaction is slight, or relates to only a small portion of the service bundle. Restaurants might horrify rather than delight customers, for example, if waiters felt compelled to comp entire meals every time a water glass was left half-filled or a roll got cold. Domino's Pizza ran into this problem with its thirty-minute-delivery-or-it's-free guarantee; some customers were uncomfortable accepting a free pizza from a huffing and puffing deliverer who was two minutes late. In these cases, reducing the payout to a level customers feel is commensurate with their dissatisfaction is probably preferable to a full refund.

- *What are the customer's true costs of failure?* A full refund doesn't compensate customers for the irritation, inconvenience, and lost time associated with an unsatisfactory product or service. Of course, these costs are intangible and vary widely from customer to customer, so putting a price on them is difficult. In addition, many companies simply can't afford to pay customers for their inconvenience on top of a full refund. But in some cases a flawed product or service can cause significant indirect expense for the customer, and a guarantee would be of little value if it didn't attempt to address these costs. Thus Prestone offers to pay up to $100 on car radiator repairs for customers using its antifreeze instead of merely returning the seven dollars or so paid for the product. And Mazda and a few other car companies provide free roadside repairs and towing to customers whose cars (higher-end models only) have broken down while under warranty. For the most part, however, uncompensated customer costs are an area that has been largely unaddressed by both product and service companies, and thus provides an opportunity to companies that wish to give added impact to guarantees and achieve higher levels of customer satisfaction.

Setting Limits

The best guarantees are simple, they protect all customers against all elements of dissatisfaction, and they are easy to invoke. Ideally, then, a customer should be able to call or approach anyone at a company, express dissatisfaction, and receive an immediate refund. Needless to say, very few guarantees meet these criteria. Some companies have good reason for restricting the scope of their guarantees: They've analyzed the costs and benefits of an unencumbered guarantee and determined that it would result in far too many unreasonable and costly triggerings. And, after all, a steady stream of unreasonable triggerings isn't in the interests of reasonable customers, since in the end they will have to share the cost of a runaway guarantee program.

Many organizations, however, burden their guarantees with limits and obstacles simply because they don't realize how such restrictions weaken a guarantee, and because they don't have enough faith in the reasonableness of the vast majority of their customers. The following questions can help companies to avoid falling into that trap:

■ *Do qualifications exclude too many customers or key sources of dissatisfaction?* The best guarantees are simple statements of a few sentences, with no small print attached. Guarantees that go on and on listing exclusions and limitations become weaker with every word—especially if the qualifications remove the company's responsibility for the very things that most irritate customers or place unreasonable demands on customers. Lufthansa, for example, guaranteed passengers that they would make connecting flights in Germany and that their baggage would arrive with them; otherwise, in either case, they would receive $200. But the guarantee went on to add the following:

> This guarantee excludes delays such as weather or air traffic control problems affecting your arrival. . . . You must, naturally, adhere to published minimum check-in times. . . . Guarantees apply to Business and First Class passengers only. . . . Trips must originate, be booked and ticketed in U.S. . . . All flights, including connecting flights, must be on Lufthansa. . . . Claims must be made in writing in U.S. within 60 days of date of occurrence. . . . Subject to government

approval. . . . This guarantee program may be terminated at any time without further notice.

It is worth noting that the published minimum check-in time for an international flight is two hours; thus customers who hadn't checked in at least two hours ahead of time couldn't invoke the guarantee, no matter what the airline did to them or their luggage. Coach-fare customers might also assume that Lufthansa doesn't feel particularly obligated to get them to Germany on time and with their luggage.

Another example of an impressive-sounding guarantee torpedoed by fine print is that of Squaw Valley USA ski resort. Its guarantee states that skiers don't have to wait in line; in the event that they do, the price of the lift ticket is refunded and the customer can ski for free for the rest of the day. But the guarantee is asterisked; the ensuing text explains that to qualify, customers have to pay a nominal charge to register as a beginner, intermediate, or expert skier, and the guarantee applies only when all the resort's lifts servicing that level of skier have an average wait of more than ten minutes. There is no mention of how a skier stuck in a lift line would be able to make such a determination; one can only assume that most skiers wouldn't bother.

- *Is the guarantee easy to invoke?* When customers believe that they are entitled to a payout under a guarantee, they shouldn't have to go through a torturous process to collect. Presumably they've already been inconvenienced, and any other unpleasantness associated with the invoking process will just add insult to injury. In addition to further irritating customers who slog through to get their refund, a difficult invoking process will discourage others from trying at all, thereby completely negating the guarantee as a means for becoming aware of errors, motivating change, and winning over dissatisfied customers.

Traveler's Advantage, a discount travel agency that collects an annual membership fee from its customers, promises to get its members the best price on any travel arrangements; otherwise, it will refund the fee and pay the difference between the price it offered and the lower one. But here's what the company asks its customers to do in order to collect: "Write us a note within thirty days of booking, describing the situation, and enclose documentation showing the specific prices, dates, destination, and type of accommodations on travel arrangements." Getting detailed, written price quotes on travel arrangements isn't always easy; why couldn't agency personnel simply ask customers to tell them who is offering the lower rate and then verify it themselves by phone? The guarantee would almost certainly carry more weight.

Even worse, consider Bank of America's guarantee of customer satisfaction with checking accounts. The bank generously promised dissatisfied customers a refund of six months' worth of checking fees; all the customer had to do to collect was . . . *close the account.* The bank later bragged that hardly any customers invoked the guarantee. No wonder! Who is going to go through the considerable trouble of closing out an account and opening a new one elsewhere just to collect on tens of dollars worth of compensation? And if any customers were determined to collect, the bank's guarantee would literally force them to jump to a competitor instead of giving the bank a chance to regain their loyalty. Because of the painful invoking procedure, an otherwise unique guarantee was rendered valueless.

▪ *Are time or usage limits overly tight?* Unlike L. L. Bean, most manufacturers are not prepared to offer lifetime guarantees on their products; nor would most service companies freely allow customers to demand compensation for a service rendered decades ago. It is thus reasonable to impose some sort of time limit on how long the guarantee is valid. In addition, manufacturers must often add usage limits, such as mileage for a car or number of copies for a copying machine, to ensure that ordinary customers don't end up subsidizing the cost of compensating a minority of customers who are exceptionally hard on the product.

Clearly, however, such limits should be kept as loose as possible to give the guarantee maximum impact. For starters, they should be at least as generous as those of competitors— and preferably more so. That's why the car companies keep upping the time/mileage ante on their warranties. Usage and time limits should also, at a minimum, meet customers' expectations of a product's quality and useful lifetime, or of the duration of time over which a service's impact is felt. Thus when Xerox found its customers thought a high-quality copy machine should run without serious problems for at least three years, the company changed its guarantee to reflect that expectation.

Many service firms probably don't have to worry about the question of time limits, since dissatisfied customers tend to complain on the spot or soon after the service is delivered. In fact, so few customers are likely to come in months or years later to complain that incorporating a time limit may not be worth the risk of weakening the guarantee. But some professional service firms might be exceptions: The threat of a triggering hanging over the firm long after the service has been delivered could represent a significant potential liability. In this case, the firm would do well to specify a reasonable time period in which the guarantee would be in effect. By the same token, some professional service firms may actually want to insist that the guarantee be triggerable only *after* a certain date or milestone, instead of before. The quality of legal or business advice, for example, may become apparent only after the recommendations have been implemented and a certain period of time has elapsed.

Is a Single Guarantee Enough?

Depending on the differences between types of customers and between different business units within the same company, it may not always make sense for a company to offer a single guarantee. Consider these questions:

- *Do customers fall into distinct groups?* Some organizations astutely recognize that they are serving several different types of customers, each of which might have significantly different needs from a guarantee. In that case, companies may want to design different guarantees for each segment, or even to offer guarantees to some and not to others. When Peerless Carpet Corporation considered offering its dealers a guarantee on delivery times, for example, the company determined that those dealers servicing the retail market placed a high value on *immediate* delivery, while dealers servicing contractors were more concerned with *reliable* delivery—that is, getting the carpet to them exactly when promised, even if the carpet couldn't be shipped for two weeks or more. Thus while a guarantee of three-day delivery would be highly valued by retail dealers, its other dealers might be completely content with a less strenuous guarantee that simply promised on-time delivery.

■ *Are guarantees important to all customers?* Companies that deal with a relatively small number of customers can consider offering guarantees on a customer-by-customer basis. These firms may opt to target guarantees only at new customers, for example, or even only at those new customers for whom, for whatever reasons, the marketing benefits of a guarantee seem particularly high or the risks of having the guarantee triggered seem particularly low. That doesn't mean that there's little point in extending a new guarantee to an existing customer: A guarantee could entice the customer to consider more expensive or riskier product lines or services. A company might selectively offer guarantees to existing customers, perhaps varying the scope and payout of the guarantee from customer to customer, or even changing the guarantee to a single customer over time as that customer's needs changed.

However, offering guarantees to selected customers only risks offending those who are left uncovered and could send a message to employees that there are second-rate customers—that is, customers not protected by a guarantee. The challenge for a company then becomes to provide a consistently high level of quality to every customer, regardless of the guarantee in force.

■ *Is the guarantee inappropriate for some business units?* A guarantee perfect for one part of a company may make no sense at all for another part. The different business units of highly diversified companies may be addressing entirely different customers with utterly different needs and priorities. In addition, quality and culture could vary tremendously across a company's divisions. If customers of the various business units are used to thinking of the particular units they deal with as distinct entities, then it could be entirely appropriate for these different units to design their own guarantees, or even to decline to offer a guarantee. However, companies that have built a powerful corporate identity that tends to overshadow the identity of individual units may run the risk of confusing or even angering customers by varying guarantees among business units. Thus while GM is able to get away with providing a stronger warranty for its highly distinct Saturn (the GM name is almost never mentioned in Saturn promotions) than it does for its other car lines, Xerox wisely chose to extend its powerful warranty across all of the company's products.

Performing the type of analysis prescribed in this chapter will greatly increase the chances of coming up with a guarantee that will impress customers and improve quality without eroding profits. Still, the uncountable peculiarities that characterize every industry, company, and customer base mean that the general principles of designing a guarantee should be regarded only as a platform from which the design process can be launched.

Even more important, the best-designed guarantee is likely to be an unmitigated disaster if a company doesn't move fast to boost its quality to a level commensurate with the satisfaction and performance promised by the guarantee. Achieving quality in concert with a guarantee program is the subject of the next chapter.

Chapter 6
Getting a Jump on Quality

Many organizations jump at the idea of offering a strong guarantee to land new business or increase market share. However, if a company is not simultaneously taking visible steps to improve its internal product manufacturing or service delivery capabilities, offering a guarantee is a marketing gimmick that will have little positive long-term impact. In fact, it may well produce a negative one: Customers could resent being misled into believing they were purchasing a high-quality product or service, and employees could become cynical about the company's commitment to quality and its customers. Meanwhile, the company will very likely be suffering a torrent of guarantee payouts.

To keep an extraordinary guarantee program from degenerating into a debacle, an organization must scrutinize its operations, searching out and plugging quality leaks. Many companies will find that they must go even further and reengineer their processes from top to bottom in order to bring quality up to the requirements of a powerful guarantee. Quality need not be extraordinary to roll out an extraordinary guarantee; after all, part of the point of introducing a powerful guarantee is to achieve that elusive level of quality. But quality should be reasonably sound. How sound? A simple litmus test is for managers to ask themselves if they truly feel comfortable with the thought of putting the company's performance on the line with an extraordinary guarantee. That's one of the remarkable properties of a powerful guarantee: Even before you put it into place, it has you thinking along the right lines.

Quality programs, of course, are not new to manufacturing

companies. But there has been a growing perception that traditional approaches to quality at most manufacturers have failed to produce anything approaching the hoped-for increases in market share, customer loyalty, or profitability. One reason is that these programs typically concentrate on such parameters as short-term cost savings, product conformance to standard specifications, or increased inventory turns. Excluded from the formula has been customer satisfaction, and that has proved to be a costly mistake. According to an article in *The Economist*, Allen-Bradley, Florida Power & Light, and British Telecom are among the companies that have dismantled or revamped massive quality improvement programs because the results were not having a positive impact on customers.[1] The Baldridge Award itself may be partly to blame for this problem; although the award emphasizes customer satisfaction, it is only one of seven key criteria for the award, with the other six focusing on internal processes. In their obsession with improving these processes, manufacturing companies have simply forgotten to ask what the customer is getting out of the improvements.

Service companies, being newer to the idea of quality improvement, don't carry this baggage; they have tended to focus on customer satisfaction from the start, if for no other reason than that it's not clear what else they could focus on. But this advantage over manufacturing companies is offset by the fact that service companies have little experience with instituting formal quality improvement programs, and hesitate to plunge into unfamiliar territory. Perhaps for this reason service companies haven't fared as well in the Baldridge Awards: The first award to a service company, Federal Express, wasn't given until 1990.

An extraordinary guarantee program forces managers to forge a link between quality improvement and customer focus. Because it will be paying out on customer dissatisfaction, a manufacturing company with an exceptional guarantee can't help but make the customer a top priority. Likewise, a service company with a guarantee has no choice but to throw itself into the world of quality improvement. Furthermore, a guarantee breaks companies of the habit of being reactive to quality problems or customer dissatisfaction because it forces them to strive not to make the errors that create dissatisfaction in the first place. Rather than clean up messes and pay out, a company will quickly learn to prevent those costly messes.

Once an extraordinary guarantee has been rolled out, it won't be long before a company finds itself frantically patching the relevant quality problems to avoid payouts. But why wait? Managers planning, or even contemplating, a guarantee would be wise to get a head start on the sorts of quality improvements that are necessary to avoid massive payouts. Generally speaking, there are three steps to take: (1) defining excellence in products and services from the customer's point of view; (2) adjusting—or even rebuilding—the processes that produce (or limit) excellence in the areas that will affect the guarantee; and (3) ensuring that employees are part of the guarantee solution, not part of the problem.

What Do Customers Want?

One way to establish quality goals is to adopt industry standards for such obvious characteristics as product reliability or service timeliness. But doing so can result in raising the bar on product or service elements that customers aren't concerned about, and ignoring those elements on which customers make their purchasing and repurchasing decisions. Thus whereas a number of clothing-oriented retailers have driven themselves into or close to bankruptcy while experimenting with various pricing and fashion strategies, Nordstrom has thrived in large part because it has made a point of maintaining a huge inventory; it stocks, for example, fifty-seven different sizes of men's shirts. Industry conventional wisdom holds that off-sizes aren't profitable, but Nordstrom, which started off as a shoe store, has long recognized that customers hate the experience of seeing an item they like and then not being able to find it in their size. Especially for a company that is introducing a powerful guarantee, failing to recognize such elements of customer satisfaction can be a costly error.

Companies making the effort to find out exactly what it is

that customers want and need from their products and services are often surprised at the results, which sometimes fly in the face of conventional industry wisdom. For example, banks in the 1980s focused most of their quality improvement efforts on developing new banking products to attract a wider range of customer. But when researchers at the University of Virginia Business School asked 800 customers what they looked for in a bank, new products ranked dead last; instead, customers chose banks on the basis of the friendliness and efficiency of tellers and managers more than on any other characteristic. Similarly, a Harvard Business School study of a health insurance company revealed that the company's efforts to speed the turnaround time of physicians' claims to under a month was a waste. Doctors review receivables only once a month, so speeding off a check in ten days rather than twenty-five was hardly noticed; instead, doctors were more concerned about claims processing accuracy.

British Airways thought it had a handle on what customers looked for from its employees—until it actually asked customers in a survey. The results showed that customers were concerned with four qualities: friendliness and courtesy; problem-solving ability; willingness to bend the rules to meet customers' needs; and ability to provide recovery from service errors. Not only were the airline's managers surprised by the high ranking of the last two qualities; they had never even thought of them as relevant characteristics.

Sometimes a company finds that although it is focusing on the right dimension of quality, it may unknowingly be operating at the wrong level of quality. In the case of First Image, a Menlo Park, California, processor of computer-generated microfilm, the level was too high: The company had been struggling to turn customer orders around within four hours, but after quizzing customers it found that most would be satisfied with twenty-four-hour service. Taking the extra time allowed First Image to cut its costs and pay more attention to other aspects of quality.

Many professional service firms, with their smaller customer bases, have the luxury of being able to assess the needs of virtually every client individually. The important elements of quality, then, can be viewed not as a rigid entity representing the average customer's demands, but as a flexible set of characteristics that can be tuned and retuned on a case-by-case basis. Taking advantage of this opportunity requires instituting a mechanism for soliciting and analyzing client needs both before the commencement of service delivery and during delivery, and of adapting the service delivery process appropriately.

If It's Broke, Fix It

Having determined which elements of quality customers value most in a product or service, companies with reason to believe that their quality in these areas is strong might consider implementing their extraordinary guarantee immediately. If a company has been working on customer-satisfaction-oriented quality for a long time, and has continually heard from customers that its efforts have been successful, there is little reason to wait.

For the great majority of companies, however, this move would be premature. These companies must raise their quality in the areas identified by customers before undertaking a guarantee. Doing so involves understanding the processes and systems that affect customer satisfaction and then making the appropriate corrections.

Sometimes the process changes mandated by a guarantee are relatively simple. For example, at JWS Technologies, an industrial gas delivery company, one of the major process changes instituted to guarantee prompt, error-free delivery was adding a second delivery shift. One bank spent two years studying customer flow and the types of transactions customers engaged in, finally determining that it could virtually eliminate bottlenecks through flexible scheduling and part-time workers. In other companies, however, processes may need more extensive alteration.

Process Change at Oakley Millwork and at Henry Ford Hospital

At the time Oakley Millwork first considered a guarantee, it had already developed its order processing, inventory management, and delivery processes to give it an order fill rate—that is, the dollar value of product shipped divided by the value of product ordered—of 99.5 percent, versus an industry average of 87 percent. Clearly, the company didn't need to completely rebuild its processes. But as rightfully proud as management was of its quality in the area of fill rate, it also recognized that, in the context of guaranteeing zero backorders, the 0.5 percent gap meant that failures were occurring and that payouts would be the inevitable result.

Oakley examined in excruciating detail where errors were creeping into its system. Among its discoveries: It sometimes took the company several days to realize that a supply shipment was overdue, by which time it was too late to contact the supplier and avoid backorders; although it knew when parts arrived from suppliers, it often didn't know when the parts would be through the milling process and available for shipment to customers; customers sometimes claimed that the order Oakley processed wasn't the order they had phoned in; inventories of some products occasionally reached dangerously low levels before anyone reordered them from the suppliers; and the low-cost suppliers with whom Oakley did some business were slower to ship products than the higher-priced suppliers would.

Having identified the problems in the processes, Oakley was able to fix them in a fairly straightforward manner without completely overhauling the processes. It started noting on its calendars when supply shipments were due so that someone would be reminded to call if the shipment hadn't arrived. It started keeping track of where each part was in the milling process so that it would have a more accurate idea of how soon parts would be ready for delivery. It started faxing orders back to customers for double-checking. It programmed its computerized inventory to automatically alert managers to low inventory levels. And it changed its policy of always dealing with the lowest-cost supplier; if it needed something fast, it paid the premium. The result was that Oakley's order fill rate jumped to 100 percent, and the guarantee boosted market share and profitability.

The radiology unit at the Henry Ford Hospital in Detroit didn't guarantee satisfaction until it was able to lick the problem of patients having to put up with long waits. To do so the hospital tracked and analyzed hundreds of instances of patients kept waiting longer than fifteen minutes. Then it made some changes in its routines: It brought in a second technician and additional volunteers to the unit during those hours in which the biggest crunches usually occurred; to deal with bottlenecks, it made employee positions more flexible, so that receptionists sometimes transported patients and technicians sometimes answered telephones; and to ease the tensions of patients who did have to wait, employees took the trouble to explain the radiology process and to answer patient questions ahead of time. After a few months, patient complaints dropped to a fraction of their previous level, and the guarantee went off without a hitch.

Software to the Rescue of a Chemical Company

Mexican chemicals manufacturer Quimobasicos was also able to isolate and fix specific process problems before implementing a guarantee. The company repeatedly found that it was allowing the inventory of its distributors to become depleted of key products, which cost these distributors sales and prompted them to consider switching to other manufacturers. To regain its distributors' confidence, the company decided to guarantee the inventory levels of the products. But first it had to figure out why its distributors were running out of product, and then how to fix the problem.

Chemicals are typically transferred from large tanks at Quimobasicos to tanker trucks and then to the customers' tanks. As it turns out, during the process the amount of chemicals transferred becomes subject to a number of vagaries, including inaccurate gauges and unreliable manual estimation techniques. In addition, the demand for some of these products—such as chemicals used in refrigeration units—tends to swing wildly according to the weather and time of year.

To fix the problems, Quimobasicos developed computer software that precisely calculates the amounts of chemicals transferred in any type of shipment and then employs these calculations to track inventory levels of each chemical at each distributor. The software is also set up to monitor the distributors' sales, adjust for seasonal and weather variations, and then compare projected demands with actual inventory levels, so that management can be alerted in advance to the need for scheduling a shipment.

How the Sales Force Can Sell Satisfaction

Some companies find that the processes most needing adjustment are not the ones that immediately draw attention. One firm that designed large software systems for its clients kept running into customer satisfaction crises; no matter how many people it threw into the project, the customer would always find something to complain about. Project costs kept escalating as the company poured more and more resources into its software efforts; yet for all its work the company wasn't developing the crucial good references it needed to expand its business.

Finally, management realized that its problems weren't the result of any real shortcomings in the systems it was building; rather, the fault lay with the sales and marketing department, which was instilling new clients with unrealistic expectations of the software development process. For instance, sales reps were telling potential clients that the systems could be built exactly to the specifications demanded by the client's senior management—without regard to the fact that management "wish lists" for software systems are virtually never implementable exactly as envisioned. Bringing the sales reps back down to earth and forcing them to warn clients about the inevitable unknowns of software projects cost an occasional sale, but it also resulted in a jump in client satisfaction.

In other cases, it is obvious which processes need fixing and how to fix them—but painful to do so. Such is often the situation at U.S. manufacturing companies that have put off major capital improvements for decades because of an emphasis on short-term profits and thus now find themselves trailing

Japanese and European competitors who are operating state-of-the-art plants. Rather than trying to wring high quality out of outmoded assembly lines, companies are often better off biting the bullet and modernizing. One reason that GE was able to offer its ninety-day unconditional guarantee on appliances was that it had invested nearly $1 billion in its factories. The company now estimates that only about one percent of its customers trigger the guarantee—a fraction of the dissatisfaction it could have expected had it not put the money into its plants.

Chrysler Embraces a Viper

The most difficult challenge a company can face in its quest to boost quality is when its problems appear to be embedded in a wide range of inadequate processes, and the means for fixing them all is neither obvious nor simple. Chrysler faced such a crisis in the late 1980s. It desperately needed to improve quality—in part because it was committed to offering warranties that are among the strongest in the industry—but doing so was clearly not just a matter of adding more modern equipment to its factories. GM had poured billions into high-tech factories in the early 1980s only to watch its quality drop and costs rise. Instead, Chrysler figured out that it had to change the way it did virtually everything. It had to reengineer its processes—toss the old out, take a clean piece of paper, and come up with entirely new ways to design and construct cars.

To prove to itself, and to the outside world, that it could be done, Chrysler in 1989 squirreled a group of top-notch designers and engineers away from corporate inertia and bureaucracy. The task was to develop a sexy, ultra-high-performance production sports car based on a model that had created a stir at an auto show that year. At first, the goal seemed impossible: to design and build a thoroughly unique car virtually from scratch in three years, instead of the five years normally required to bring even a run-of-the-mill automobile from concept to assembly line.

Under pressure to find some way to speed up the process, the production team borrowed a trick from jetliner and submarine designers: It set up a computerized project management system that tracked the 900 separate major tasks involved in developing a production car, as well as the resources required to complete each task. Over the course of the project, responsibility for each of these activities was distributed to team members, so that each member could keep track of whether or not each activity was being completed on schedule. Every other week the entire team met to report any delays; the delays were then plugged into the software, which calculated what adjustments had to be made to keep the project on track. Thus if a wheel engineer came in and announced that he had a problem, the program would identify which teams and tasks were affected in what way, so that these groups could plan around the problem.

The group also pulled together a data base that tracked every design issue related to the car. That one data base became a source of information to engineers, managers, suppliers, purchasers, and anyone else who came into contact with the project. As a result, nothing ever slipped between the cracks. When a sun visor failed a durability test, the purchaser and manufacturer were immediately brought in to help the team come up with a replacement—fast. The result of these efforts was the Viper, which rolled off the assembly line right on schedule in 1992. The Viper has been winning the sort of accolades from car enthusiasts that Detroit hears all too seldom these days, and Chrysler is now moving to incorporate many of the Viper process innovations into all its car development projects.

Letting the Suppliers Do It: The Case of Kmart

In some cases, a better approach to quality is overlooked despite—or perhaps because of—its overarching simplicity. Kmart discovered one such approach when it confronted the range of processes that comprised its inventory control. Customer surveys in large department stores always indicate that the availability of merchandise is one of the two most important factors in determining where people will shop (the other is price). To ensure that they are well-stocked with the right items—and not overloaded with clunkers—Kmart and other department store chains have spent years and hundreds of millions of dollars developing more and more advanced computerized systems to track inventory and purchasing so as to be able to anticipate customer demand and send out orders to suppliers before inventory reaches dangerously low levels. But Kmart realized that this approach wasn't good enough; no matter how complex the systems, the company still sometimes failed to have the right amount of stock on its shelves.

So the company took a radically different tack: It told its key suppliers that it was no longer even going to try to anticipate customer demand; in fact, it was dispensing with the ordering process altogether. Instead, its suppliers would be responsible for managing Kmart's inventory, by monitoring customer demand for their products at each store via purchase data fed from Kmart's computers, and then shipping the right amount of product. Thus Quaker State would have to determine when a surge in demand was likely to deplete Kmart's inventory of its motor oil, and Rubbermaid would decide how large a shipment would keep Kmart's shelves filled with kitchen trash bins without hogging costly warehouse space. The plan worked beautifully: Not surprisingly, suppliers are much better at analyzing supply and demand for a handful of their products than Kmart could ever hope to be at keeping track of thousands of products.

Here is another example of broadening the notion of quality contributors: When PRISM, the pest exterminator, rethought its processes, it realized that customers had to be made part of the quality process if the company was going to realize its goal of guaranteed pest eradication. Instead of continually sending out its service people to react to recurring problems, its contract requires customers to maintain exceptionally clean facilities. Although the pest control industry had always ignored the customer's role, without customer participation pest eradication would have been virtually impossible.

Staying on Top of Errors

After a company has altered or rebuilt its processes to raise quality, it must still take steps to make sure that quality stays high. If it doesn't, the company's efforts will fall prey to the second law of thermodynamics, which holds that systems tend to move toward disorder unless energy is spent to fight the trend. When a company institutes an extraordinary guarantee, it is installing the most powerful possible safeguard against backsliding into low quality and customer dissatisfaction; transgressions will quickly translate into triggerings, providing error feedback and the motivation to fix errors. The key to making this feedback useful, and not merely tortuously costly, is to tie it into a correction loop. It's essential to lay the groundwork for that process before rolling out a guarantee.

The cornerstone of a correction loop is a flow of error data—in other words, the ability to become aware of customer dissatisfaction, and preferably on as close to a real-time, case-by-case basis as possible. In the absence of a guarantee, this can be a difficult chore, and one that many companies ignore entirely—especially service companies, which traditionally have not instituted formal processes for keeping track of screw-ups the way manufacturing companies track product returns, or the way their own accounting departments keep track of every dime spent.

One consulting company, for example, found that client complaints often did not make it up from account reps to management for weeks at a time, and even then it was sometimes several more weeks before action was taken on the complaint. After losing an account over an unaddressed complaint, the company ordered all its account reps to report any complaints to the head office by the end of the day. Every morning, management would meet for up to two hours to determine how each and every complaint would be addressed.

Manpower, Inc., which hires out temporary secretarial and other help, phones every customer within two days of placing a temp to find out if there are any problems. When the placement is over, the company sends the customer a questionnaire that attempts to identify exactly the areas in which the person who was placed might have lacked a necessary skill, as well as those in which he or she might have excelled. The purpose of the data isn't so much to uncover incompetent employees—employees are well-screened ahead of time—but rather to improve Manpower's ability to match employees to customer needs, so that it can avoid leaving customers feeling shortchanged or wasting an employee with exceptional skills on a routine placement.

In the absence of a strong guarantee, many customers need convincing that a company is truly interested in hearing about their dissatisfaction. A little creative complaint solicitation can help. British Airways set up videotaping booths outside its arriving flights and invited passengers to step in for a moment to air their complaints before the camera, with the assurance that the tape would be reviewed by management. The Maine Savings Bank of Portland offered customers one dollar for every complaint letter; although the payment was a token one that could hardly be seen as compensation for any but the most trivial of slights, the gesture communicated the bank's eagerness to hear about its errors.

If the error-collection-and-correction loop is tight enough, problems can be ferreted out and corrected before a large number of customers become dissatisfied—or before a small number of customers become extremely dissatisfied to the point of wanting to tell the world, thereby negating the goodwill of a thousand times as many fully satisfied customers. Microfilm processor First Image maintains no less than seventy-five categories of errors for its output, ranging from obvious slipups such as poor image quality to easily overlooked goofs such as misaligned film-edge slits or inaccurate delivery. All these error data are religiously fed into a computer data base and then organized into the form of easily digested graphs that are printed out and studied; any hint of a trend toward slippage in a category is immediately addressed.

Likewise, hotel chain Hampton Inn recognized that its customer satisfaction guarantee would be a disaster if it didn't keep a close eye on the myriad ways in which a guest can become irritated in the course of a night's stay. Thus the company regularly conducts quality "audits" in which an employee registers as a guest at one of the hotels without revealing his or her identity. After the visit—which included a staged complaint—the employee fills out a form that poses several hundred questions about the quality of the service and facilities. Some examples: "Did the hotel answer within five rings when calling for a reservation?" "Did the lettering on the advertising billboards outside look professional?" "After the complaint was resolved did the front desk call back to make sure the problem had been solved to your satisfaction?" "Did employees have eye-to-eye contact with you?" Companies that keep this tight a grip on quality maintenance are unlikely to let disaffected customers catch them by surprise.

The People Factor

No matter how well-thought-out a company's processes are, quality will remain inadequate if employees lack the skill, training, or motivation to rigorously execute them. The importance of employee execution is particularly obvious when identical systems have been installed in similar operating units of the company, and yet unit performance varies widely. Club Med, for example, runs its various resorts in much the same way; yet customer satisfaction ratings often range far above and below the company average of 85 percent. This sort of variance is related to hard-to-define qualities such as personal leadership, team spirit, morale, and an internalized desire to maintain high standards of excellence.

Many quality improvement programs, while embraced by management, fail to make it down to the rank and file. In large part, this is because most such programs are centrally managed and attempt to impose motivation and buy-in in a sort of trickle-down fashion. In addition, quality programs usually aim for slow, continuous improvement, a goal that doesn't lend itself to inspiration and enthusiasm.

An extraordinary guarantee, on the other hand, solves much of the problem by acting as an organizational supercharger. It can literally impose a state of crisis on an organization—a crisis that calls for commitment on the part of everyone in the company. When a powerful guarantee is in effect, frontline employees are no longer mere cogs in the wheel; they are suddenly in a position to make or break the company, as guarantee payouts balloon or shrivel with their efforts. When JWS Technologies implemented its guarantee, for example, stock-pulling errors shrank from 4 percent to 0.5 percent, even though the stock-pulling procedures remained largely the same.

Before rolling out a guarantee, management should try to get a head start on cultivating in employees the appropriate attitude and commitment to customer satisfaction that are necessary to the success of the guarantee. One organization that has been successful in instilling employees with the desire and ability to satisfy customers—though it offers no formal guarantee—is Disneyworld. From the moment they join the resort, employees are referred to as "cast members," whether they entertain in dance halls or sweep streets. All employees attend "Disney U," where they learn about the history and traditions of the company, in addition to the details of their jobs—the ticket-taking course is thirty-two hours long—and also have a chance to take classes in nonjob-related subjects such as languages, accounting, and dancing. Everyone from the president of the company to the popcorn vendors wears a first-name-only name tag. In large part because of the way such policies breed top-to-bottom commitment to customer satisfaction, Disneyworld is one of those rare organizations for which an extraordinary guarantee would be utterly superfluous.

It can be a difficult task to convince employees that when it comes to customer satisfaction, it is no longer business as usual; at many companies employees have become cynical about management fads. Every organization will have to develop a unique approach to overcoming this resistance. Speedy Muffler King, for example, held a two-and-a-half-day conference attended by both senior management and 600 local managers to discuss quality issues; the mere expense and logistical difficulties of such an event can help demonstrate to employees that a reordering of priorities is taking place. At the Hotel Sonesta in Boston, employees practice responding to customer problems through role-playing and then rate each other's responses according to how observant and caring they were and how effectively they solved the customer's problem or compensated the customer for any unresolved dissatisfaction. One bellhop who had participated in the training was approached late one night by a guest who wanted to know where he might purchase a belt, having left his at home. There wasn't any place to buy a belt at that hour, but the bellhop hesitated only a second before yanking off his own belt and offering it to the stunned but grateful guest.

Because an extraordinary guarantee can have such a strong impact on the company's financial picture, and because employees have such a strong impact on the success of the guarantee, it is only reasonable that employees be compensated generously in parallel with any gains the company makes via the guarantee. This is hardly a radical notion; more than half of the companies in a survey performed by the consulting firm Handy HRM reported that they link, or will shortly be linking, some salaries to various measures of quality, including customer satisfaction. Linking compensation and customer satisfaction is especially crucial for a company whose profitability is on the line because of a powerful guarantee. Some companies will find that they will also want to—or have to—increase base compensation to ensure that they are attracting and holding the sort of top-notch people who can make the difference between a guarantee that takes off and a guarantee that blows up. Landscape maintenance firm Chemlawn, for example, ignores the industry cost-saving practice of relying on part-time help for its seasonal business and hires primarily full-time employees whom it trains. It's an expensive policy, but as a result, Chemlawn is able to promise—and charge for—better service to its customers.

In short, a company that raises its quality and its customer satisfaction sensitivity to a level high enough to allow offering an extraordinary guarantee has already achieved much of the benefit of the guarantee before even rolling it out. The very process of considering what it takes to offer a powerful guarantee is eye-opening, even frightening; it's also enough in many cases to make an organization take the steps it probably should have taken long before to start ensuring customer satisfaction. Even if a company decides that an extraordinary guarantee isn't in the cards after all, just going through the motions of thinking through the quality and customer satisfaction issues can make the experience of considering a guarantee a highly profitable one.

But whether a company has succeeded in lifting its quality to the level of a guarantee, or has stalled out short of its goal, there is one more step it can take to improve its outlook. This step can serve to raise quality yet another notch, and at the same time help to familiarize a company with many of the issues related to rolling out an extraordinary guarantee. The next chapter describes this step in detail.

Note

1. "The Cracks in Quality," *The Economist,* April 18, 1991, p. 67.

Chapter 7

Internal Guarantees

Most organizations are all too familiar with the walls that spring up between departments and functions. Whether caused by lack of communication, a failure to provide or share sufficient resources, or personal friction, the symptoms of intraorganizational inertia are many and conspicuous. Any one of the following scenarios may play itself out:

- A product development team working on a critical project is months past deadline, apparently spinning its wheels.

- The human resources department seems unable to take fast, effective action in filling critical managerial and staff job vacancies.

- Marketing people promise product features and delivery dates that other departments cannot deliver on, leading to customer dissatisfaction as well as internal conflicts.

- Employees come up with creative excuses for not attending training courses that management has ostensibly developed for their benefit. Managers come up with creative excuses for postponing performance appraisals. And everyone comes up with creative excuses for missing meetings that never start when scheduled, leaving highly paid people twiddling their thumbs or drifting back to their offices.

- Managers deliberately pad their budgets and schedules to compensate for the internal delays and snafus they have come to see as inevitable.

Such problems can be viewed as a failure of "internal quality"—that is, as quality glitches that have a more direct impact on the functioning of the organization than on external customers. That's not to say that these glitches can't cause serious problems with regard to customers; in fact, as internal problems multiply and become more severe, they almost always manifest themselves in ways that cost a company business. But at least in the initial stages, internal quality issues are best treated at their sources within the organization.

Just as an external guarantee can go a long way toward improving a company's standing with external customers, an internal guarantee—a guarantee made by one group of employees to another group of employees in the same company—can provide a dramatic solution to persistent internal quality problems.

The basic form and concept of internal guarantees are similar to those of external guarantees. There are also differences. The most obvious difference is that while an external guarantee is a promise made by a business to its customers, an internal guarantee is a promise of superior service (timeliness, accuracy, feedback, courtesy, or whatever is at issue) made by a department to its internal customers, the people to whom its work moves next, or whom it serves in a support function. On an assembly line, a worker's internal customer might be the next worker on the line; in a service company, a worker might have just one internal customer or several (the printing department may serve the entire organization).

Another difference between internal and external guarantees is that internal guarantees are a more universally applicable solution. As mentioned earlier, not all companies are in a position to offer external guarantees; some companies have nothing to gain from one, while others are simply not prepared to offer quality sufficiently high to minimize the risk of paying out on promises not kept. The internal guarantee, by contrast, is applicable to virtually *all* companies, whatever their current level of internal or external quality. Rare indeed is the company with no suboptimal internal processes, or the company that can't afford the slight risks entailed by an internal guarantee.

Even organizations that have worked hard on process improvement—whether through Total Quality Management (TQM), crossfunctional teams, process mapping, value engineering, or similar initiatives—probably still suffer from a number of internal kinks and headaches not addressed by these improvement programs. Just as external guarantees help highlight and solve problems that directly lead to customer dissatisfaction, internal guarantees highlight and solve problems that lead to intraorganizational dissatisfaction and inefficiency. Ultimately, the results of solving these internal difficulties will have a positive impact on customers.

Before discussing the components of effective internal guarantees and providing examples of their workings, let's examine the nature of internal customers.

Defining the Internal Customer

Ironically, even companies that have wholeheartedly adopted a customer service orientation often overlook the importance of satisfying internal customers. The first step in addressing this oversight is to recognize who those customers are. It is thought-provoking, if not surprising, that many employees when asked to identify their internal customer name their boss. Clearly, most organizations still reward employees primarily for satisfying their supervisors rather than for satisfying the needs of the other employees they are actually there to serve (though one might argue that, ultimately, all employees are there to serve the external customer, no matter how indirectly).

The concept of internal customers is hardly new. The idea dates back to the 1970s, when IBM CEO Thomas Watson declared as one of his basic management beliefs that everyone in a company works for everybody else. The employees of a company that embraces this attitude do not "throw their work over the wall" at some unknown "them" when they complete it. They recognize, in a very real sense, that design and development work for production, that people on the factory floor work for the people in sales and shipping, and that finance and administration work for everyone else. Ideally, every worker understands how his or her job fits into the long chain of functions that, together, constitute the work of the organization and determine its success.

One way to grasp the internal customer concept is to consider each department or support function as an independent contractor to the departments it serves, as if it were operating in a free marketplace rather than as a box fixed forever in concrete on the organizational chart. As an independent contractor facing free market competition, a department would have to provide consistently good service at a reasonable price, or it would be out the door.

Few companies' departments take this attitude. People are often complacent in their jobs. Internal customers are generally captive buyers with no alternatives, and end up frustrated by what they see as a lack of support from their internal service providers. Employees are usually juggling different priorities; if the boss emphasizes getting the paperwork done rather than satisfying the next worker on the line, requests from internal customers may come to seem like interruptions to an employee's "real" work. In some cases, internal customers are actually perceived as a kind of enemy rather than as partners in the organization's work. This is demonstrated by the frequency of interdepartmental clashes. Worst of all, the costs of poor internal quality are often not easily quantified, so few managers recognize how damaging it actually is. Thus simply creating awareness of internal customer relationships can be a potent first step toward ironing out long-standing operating wrinkles. An internal guarantee can then be the second step.

The Basic Form of the Internal Guarantee

Here are a few generic examples of how internal guarantees might be formulated:

> "Our department will not exceed our cost estimate for providing you with [*the specified services*]; if we do, we'll absorb all extra costs."
> "Our department will meet the deadline that we have mutually agreed upon for [*the project*]; if not, we will inform your external customers of the reasons for the

delay, and reduce your charge for the project by 20 percent."

"Maintenance/repair orders will be fulfilled within two working days. If not, we will let you know within twelve hours of receiving your order when the order *can* be completed, and work with you to determine an acceptable substitute, short-term solution to the problem you reported."

Internal guarantees can be applied to problems both big and small. Sometimes it's the smallest vexations that create the most ill will between departments; these can be quickly cleared up with an internal guarantee. For example, if internal customers usually have to wait several minutes for the provider department's phone to be answered, and often give up in frustration, the provider might promise that all calls will be answered by the fourth ring, or that voice mail messages will be returned within fifteen minutes.

One consulting firm set up a "clean desk" guarantee: All desks must be left in an orderly state at the end of the day, or the offender must pay a 25-cent fine into an office entertainment fund. A clean desk may sound like a trivial matter, but the company believed that neatness helped cultivate an atmosphere of professionalism and efficiency. As an important bonus, some managers discovered that their inability to keep their desks clean indicated that they had fundamental problems with the way they organized their work and information. Addressing these more basic flaws automatically helped clear up the desks and improved the overall performance of these managers.

In addressing a more significant and widespread problem, one manufacturing company established an on-time meeting guarantee: Anyone who appeared late for a meeting had to pay $100 to every other person in the room. A steep penalty? Yes, but not compared with the cost of having top-salary executives waste their time waiting for a meeting to start.

The Elements of a Good Guarantee

Unlike external guarantees, internal guarantees tend to be more powerful when they promise specific levels of performance rather than unconditional satisfaction. That's because an employee, unlike an external customer, is generally hesitant about claiming personal dissatisfaction with another employee's work. To ensure an appropriate rate of triggerings, an internal guarantee should base triggerings on conditions that can be measured in relatively objective ways, so that personal concerns don't enter into the equation. Thus it is preferable to promise "completion of work orders within two business days" rather than the more elastic "prompt service." In addition, the performance measure on which triggerings are based should be one that is deemed important by the internal customer.

Of course, the guarantee should provide for a payout of some kind when the promise is not met. The payout need not be of a financial nature so long as it gives the guarantee teeth. Additionally, as with external guarantees, there should be a clearly understood and simple procedure for invoking the guarantee, as well as a mechanism for tracking how often the guarantee is not met, so that the organization can learn from the guarantee process.

It is vital to note that although the internal guarantee may look like the familiar "performance standards" set by managers, it differs in several ways. Clearly, one difference is the payout, which provides a constant incentive to improve; ordinarily there is no established penalty for failing to meet a standard. People still show up late for meetings even when a company has forcefully stated that meetings must begin on time. But how many managers will repeat the mistake of showing up late when they have to hand over $100 to each of the seven people kept waiting? Few people at the manufacturing company that instituted this guarantee policy doubted that they would have to make good on the payout—especially after the president himself showed up late for a meeting and coughed up the penalty.

When a run-of-the-mill performance standard is not met, management typically punishes departments or individuals for the failure, which may jolt people out of their easy chairs in the short term. But most often the blame for a failure rests not with individuals but with a company's systems and processes; blaming people for problems beyond their control only savages morale. Additionally, a common employee reaction to management censure for failing to meet a standard is simply to come up with excuses or to blame other people or departments. By contrast, when a group of employees fails to live up to a guarantee with a penalty attached, employees and managers can pay the penalty without humiliation and then search out the root causes of the problem or problems and come up with real solutions—not Band-Aids or excuses—that will enable them to avoid further penalties.

Another way in which the internal guarantee differs from a performance standard is that it is developed *jointly* by the internal service provider and the internal customer. A performance standard, by contrast, is typically promulgated in top-down fashion by management, without any input from those who must meet it. Thus it often shows no understanding of the barriers that may make the standard impossible to achieve, and even no knowledge of whether the standard is important to internal customers.

Companies That Have Implemented Internal Guarantees

Although the idea of instituting formal internal guarantees is a relatively new one, a few companies have aggressively pioneered their use. The results strongly suggest that internal guarantees can live up to their promise.

Westinghouse

Internal guarantees allowed Westinghouse to attack long-standing problems between its individual business units (IBUs) and its R&D arm, the Science and Technology Center (STC). Historically, STC offered "best-guess" estimates of project timetables and costs, often ran over budget and behind schedule, and left its internal customers in the dark about project progress while wrestling in isolation with development problems.

In considering an internal guarantee, Westinghouse corporate executives and STC investigated the root causes of stalled, botched, and budget-busting R&D projects. It soon became clear that the glitches stemmed largely from the inadequate specifications provided to STC by the IBUs at the inception stage; the IBUs would dump a job on the table without fully developing the idea or identifying their precise needs, and then grow frustrated as projects bogged down in STC's continual redefining and rethinking. Communication was poor, and made worse by the growing mutual frustration between STC and its customers.

To address this problem, STC conceived the following three-part guarantee for its internal customers:

1. Customers are to be kept advised of the cost and progress of an R&D project so that they can decide whether or not to continue the project.
2. STC agrees not to exceed costs on a project without prior customer approval.
3. If a change in project design or execution is required because of a mistake or miscalculation by STC, STC will pay the difference. For example, if the original project design specifies a particular component and it doesn't work correctly, STC will absorb the cost of the new component.

At first glance, it may look as though this guarantee places all the risk and responsibility on STC and none on the IBUs. But in actuality, to fulfill the guarantee and avoid the payouts, STC had to ask for more cooperation from the IBUs in articulating their requirements from square one. STC and its customers had to sit down at the beginning of each project and plan their goals together, in a nonconfrontational way, intercepting potential problems and misunderstandings before individual egos were put on the line.

The results of this strengthened partnership were striking. STC scientists proved able to deliver accurate cost estimates and to meet customer requirements far more effectively than before. Lines of communication opened up not only at a project's inception but throughout the life of the project, as customers were kept informed of project progress and problems rather than in the dark as before.

Although the STC promise to pay for its mistakes has only rarely been invoked, it has had a significant effect on STC's processes. If a new component is required to replace STC's first choice, for example, STC must go to the corporate level for the money to pay for it rather than simply bill the IBU customer, as in the past. This means that if STC is to avoid going to corporate with its hat in its hand, it must meet the agreed-upon specs. In addition, corporate gains valuable information about how often, and why, projects run into trouble—the sort of feedback loop that is essential to continuous improvement.

Creative Personal Services

One company that offers an example of how an internal guarantee can help solve an external problem is direct mail firm Creative Professional Services (CPS). CPS's printed materials often failed to meet its external customers' requirements, leading to dissatisfaction, costly rework, and late deliveries. Because the production department was historically seen as the cause of the problem, management initially considered having that department offer an external guarantee.

A more careful examination of the situation, however, revealed that the root cause of bungled orders rested with the salespeople, who did not always provide complete and accurate specs to production when handing over a print order. Salespeople's job orders came in all forms, including handwritten sheets that were sometimes illegible or error-ridden or covered with Post-it Notes. There was no formal, standardized system for ensuring that all relevant specs were captured from external customers before orders were placed in the production hopper.

As a result, it seemed more appropriate for the salespeople to offer an internal guarantee to their internal customers, the production people. Sales then asked production, in essence, "What would you like us to guarantee for you?" The answer: "complete, accurate information at the time a job order is placed." CPS then developed a standardized "launch form" to be used for all production orders, with blanks for every conceivable spec and a checklist to ensure that all relevant information was gathered from external customers at one time.

With this form to shore up the internal process, the sales/ account people offered production the following guarantee: "We will provide you with ALL the information you need to do each job right and on deadline. If not, we will take you to lunch, sing a song at your next department meeting, or enter any missing specs into the computer ourselves." (Note that a payout need not entail a heavy financial penalty and that it can even encompass an element of fun.)

CPS began its internal guarantee process with a trial run and tracked the results. During the trial period there were fifty invocations of the guarantee, thirty-two of them for incomplete information, eighteen for inaccurate information. Analyzing these invocations allowed CPS to identify the most common root causes of problems and thus to take the first step toward eliminating them. The guarantee program has already made a sizable dent in an old, irritating problem and has also yielded "softer" benefits in the form of changed attitudes. After the trial run, for example, one CPS supervisor apologized to the production staff for having chewed them out over errors; instead, he said, he would henceforth thank them for bringing errors to his attention.

The guarantee also brought about an attitude change among the production workers. Not only had they long been the scapegoat for screwups, but they had no direct contact with external customers, and were therefore not "heroes" even when a project fully met a customer's expectations. All this changed after the internal guarantee was implemented. In this way, internal guarantees can help make those at the "back of the house" more aware that they are an essential link in the long chain of company functions that culminate in customer satisfaction.

GTE

Internal guarantees are especially well suited to strengthening functions that are crucial to the organization over the long run but that don't leave immediate, visible scars if overlooked for a while. One such haphazardly managed function is training and development.

Recognizing the problem, GTE Mobile Communications established a guarantee that promises every single employee a minimum of forty hours of in-house formal training each year, or the employee can take forty hours of external training courses at company expense. The point of this guarantee is to ensure that GTE does not fall into the usual trap of neglecting training either when budgets are tight or when rapid company growth forces a concentration on filling job openings rather than on developing existing human resources. The considerable expense of subsidizing outside training is one reason that this guarantee provides strong motivation for in-house training. In addition, the company will obviously reap more benefit from developing its employees in its own way in the subjects and skills most important to the company's mission and needs.

Another internal guarantee is offered by GTE's Management Education and Training Department: "We guarantee that you will be satisfied with any course delivered at the GTE Management Development Center (MDC), or we will refund your tuition and room and board." All too often, companies offer "nice-to-know" classes or readily available canned courses, without seriously considering their usefulness to managers and employees; managers and employees, in turn, often find such training a waste of time. Also, managers rarely follow up with employees to determine whether the training offered was of real benefit, and delivered in an exciting, relevant way by the best possible faculty. Short, rote, multiple-choice course evaluation forms rarely provide real answers to these questions.

The training guarantee forced GTE's MDC to ask itself, as well as its customers, how well it was really serving employees' needs. Did the training offer information they could actually use? Did it prepare them in any way for advancement? Were the instructors and materials effective, the training facilities adequate and conducive to learning, the class schedule appropriate? The guarantee is communicated in writing not just to employees but also to all GTE faculty, underscoring GTE's commitment to effective training. Instructors are put on notice that if they deliver lackluster, disorganized, or irrelevant courses, they will not be invited back.

The guarantee has been invoked for reasons ranging from instructor incompetence to oversized classes to misleading course descriptions. To date, these guarantee payouts have cost GTE about $11,000—a piddling amount compared to the value of the information gained about improving course offerings in the future. As a result, GTE has now rolled out the guarantee in all its training facilities around the world.

Marriott Bethesda

Personal recruitment is another area that is often accorded too little respect or attention, despite its potential for helping an organization reach its goals. All too often, however, HR people are hamstrung by low-impact but unavoidable busywork, filling out an endless stream of forms and dealing with ever-changing government labor regulations and other administrative minutiae. For these reasons, the Human Resource Department (HRD) at the Marriott Bethesda Hotel turned to internal guarantees to force the department to focus on the most pressing needs of its internal customers.

The hotel was experiencing dramatic growth at the time, but HRD was awash in benefits issues, salary restructuring, and legal paperwork. In the crush of these matters, the HRD manager realized, his department has lost sight of its fundamental purpose: hiring qualified people. Key jobs were going vacant for too long. The manager developed three guarantees, based on the three areas determined to be of greatest concern to HRD's internal customers:

1. Job applicants will receive an interview with the appropriate department within thirty minutes of the initial screening interview. Applicants who must wait longer will be given a complimentary dinner for two in the hotel restaurant.
2. HRD guarantees to find and refer qualified applicants to departments within two weeks of receiving a job

requisition. If this guarantee is not met, the position
will be filled with a temporary worker at the expense of
the Human Resource Department.
3. Employees who find a payroll or benefit error on their
paychecks will receive a complimentary dinner for two.

These guarantees—framed on the manager's wall—served
the purpose of focusing HR's attention on customer needs and
establishing mutually agreed-upon performance standards.
The guarantees succeeded in accelerating the recruiting and
hiring processes without compromising them. As with all
internal guarantees, the payout provisions created an incentive
for improvement while also providing a formal means of tracking errors. The results have been gratifying to HRD and its
internal customers alike. Before the guarantees were developed, the hotel had an average of forty-five job openings at any
given time; afterward, that number dropped to four.

Getting Started

Developing internal guarantees is a less involved process than
developing external guarantees; in fact, it is less involved than
most quality-improvement schemes. It does not require a
twelve-point strategic plan or layers upon layers of management to design or implement, and although more staffing or
equipment is sometimes necessary to make a guarantee feasible, long-standing problems can frequently be solved at little
or no cost. Given this attractive cost/benefit ratio, the relevant
question for management is probably not, "Why should we
offer internal guarantees?" but rather, "Why not? What have
we got to lose?"

As we have seen, internal guarantees can be applied to
virtually every function in an organization, and management
may ultimately want everyone to offer a guarantee as part of a
teamwork chain that produces breakthrough levels of quality.
Ordinarily, however, a company may prefer to start with a few
pilot projects, which, properly handled, will generate results
and momentum.

As with any quality-related initiative, it is important to choose the first candidates for internal guarantees carefully. The success or failure of pilot guarantees determines how readily the rest of the organization will accept the guarantee concept. Should you start with your biggest problem area, with a high-performing function already capable of living up to the most stringent guarantee, or with something in between? Some of the factors you should weigh in determining the most appropriate internal process to concentrate on first are these: What is the frequency of the problem, and its impact? To what extent is the process out of control? What resources (in dollars, management time, and employee time) will it take to eradicate the root causes of the problem? Are there political issues or sensitivities to consider? What would the payoff be, internally and externally, for solving the problem?

There are no hard-and-fast rules about the best place to start—except this one: Don't begin by sticking a guarantee on a hopelessly quality-starved function. To do so is to invite failure and keep the internal guarantee concept from gaining organizational acceptance. A function that is truly out of control might be a better candidate for radical reengineering.

Determining the payout is another tricky issue. The most obvious type of payout is a cash payout, but care must be taken. First of all, employees should generally not be required to make payments out of their own pockets. (The $100 late-to-meeting fine discussed earlier is exceptional because managers usually have complete personal control over whether or not they can be on time for a meeting.) Should payments come out of department or corporate funds? Should they be token payments or large enough to inflict real pain?

In most cases, employees don't really want more cash for their departments; they just want the work done right. That's why First Tennessee Bank incorporated payouts of just five dollars into its set of internal guarantees. And many companies choose to forgo cash payments altogether in favor of symbolic payouts such as free dinners. In any case, the payout should, if at all feasible, provide some incentive for having the offending department correct its errors.

A department's internal guarantee is a bold announcement

of its commitment to eliminate a problem, and internal customers can't help but respond favorably. The guarantee also serves
as a rallying cry for the providers—a declaration of war on
poor quality, with a built-in penalty for defeat. A company
with appropriate internal guarantees in place will have a far
better chance of succeeding with higher-profile, higher-payoff,
and higher-risk external guarantees. As a bonus, designing
and implementing internal guarantees can serve as practice for
bringing out an external guarantee—a challenge I discuss in
the next chapter.

Chapter 8
Rolling Out the Guarantee

Having designed a guarantee, and having made an effort to raise quality at least to the level where it won't turn the guarantee into a fiasco, a company must now face the task of preparing to formally introduce the guarantee. This step may call for considerable effort: Rolling out an extraordinary guarantee is not just a matter of printing up cards and taping them to the cash register.

There are three key elements to implementing a guarantee: (1) setting up the mechanisms that provide for triggering, paying out on, and recording data on the guarantee; (2) preparing employees for the guarantee; and (3) communicating the guarantee to customers to maximize its impact. If any of these implementation steps is given short shrift, the potential power of an extraordinary guarantee can be short-circuited, resulting, perhaps after an initial flurry of enthusiasm, in business as usual—or worse.

Placing a Finger on the Trigger

Perhaps the single greatest mistake that companies trying their hands at guarantees make is to fail to set forth a clear and inviting mechanism for triggering the guarantee. Many companies assume that customers who really want to trigger the guarantee will find some way to do so. Others may believe that the purpose of the guarantee is to attract and reassure customers, and that triggering is a nuisance; these companies may actually hope that customers will be discouraged from triggering the guarantee. Either way, the power of the guarantee will be severely undercut.

Unless a company has achieved very high levels of customer satisfaction, it should *want* its guarantee to be triggered because it is through the act of guarantee invocation that dissatisfied customers will be brought back into the fold, and that the company will learn about its quality leaks. But guarantees will only be triggered if there is a clear, simple mechanism for doing so. Otherwise, the typical dissatisfied customer is inclined simply to take his or her business elsewhere rather than go through any further inconvenience to receive compensation.

Pan Am and Continental, two airlines not perceived as dedicated to customer satisfaction in the first place, both made this sort of error when they introduced money-back guarantees of satisfaction with the purchase of certain first-class tickets. To trigger the guarantee, customers first had to find an airline service agent, which might involve traveling around the airport and waiting in line to do so, and then to fill out a long claim form and submit it with photocopies of their tickets and boarding passes. Then, assuming that their claim was approved, they had to wait four to six weeks for reimbursement. The high-powered business travelers at whom this guarantee was aimed were not likely to be particularly impressed with the eventual compensation, even if they took the trouble to get the form and churn out the paperwork; they'd have long since switched airline loyalty by the time the check arrived. Such a guarantee, then, can degenerate into the worst of both worlds: It costs the company money without winning customer loyalty.

Or take the guarantee McDonald's introduced in 1992: It promised fast service and hot food, among other things, or the restaurant would "make it right." If it didn't make it right, stated the guarantee, the customer would get a coupon for a free meal. But how is McDonald's supposed to make it right for a customer who receives slow service? By the time the customer complains of slow service, the damage is done; it would make sense for reimbursement to follow immediately. As a practical matter, routines varied from unit to unit and even from server to server, but in general customers suffering through slow service were simply told that the food would be served shortly. Even customers who experienced egregiously slow service typically had to *insist* on a free meal coupon to receive one. The problem was that there was no clear mechanism for ensuring that a slighted customer would get the coupon with a minimum of fuss. Although some servers were in fact quick to provide inconvenienced customers with freebies, most customers who experienced slow service or other problems suffered in resigned silence.

By contrast, consider the guarantee offered by Mexican chemical manufacturer Quimobasicos, which told its distributor customers that if the company's failure to maintain distributor inventory levels resulted in a lost sale, the distributor had only to pick up the phone and report the amount of profits it had lost out on; Quimobasicos would then immediately put a check in the mail for that amount, without so much as a cursory effort to verify the size, or even the existence, of the claimed lost sale.

For some companies, making it easy for customers to invoke the guarantee isn't enough. Some Acura car dealerships, for example, solicit triggerings of their repair service guarantee by calling customers a few days after the service is performed to see if any problems have come to light; if so, the dealership usually takes care of them at no cost to the customer. JWS Technologies goes even further: In the event it violates its promise of error-free gas delivery, it triggers its guarantee itself, even if the customer had no intention of doing so (see Figure 8-1). And PRISM, which offers a pass-through compensation of a free meal to bug-spotting patrons of its customer restaurants, actually stipulates in its contracts that restaurants must *insist* that patrons accept the free meal.

Most guarantees create a gray area in which a customer might feel entitled to reimbursement, even though the claim could be legitimately denied on a technicality. It is crucial that companies decide ahead of time that they will routinely resolve such ambiguities in favor of the customer. The money saved in payouts by looking for excuses not to pay is far outweighed by the ill will earned from such stubbornness. For example, many high-quality manufacturers, such as Hewlett-Packard and Toy-

Figure 8-1.   Customers of Blue Valley Welding Supply (sister company to JWS Technologies, Inc.) are handed one of these certificates when their delivery is late.

I guess you think we belong in the Dog House

. . . for missing that delivery, eh? You're right, we do.

We're sorry for the inconvenience, and hope it's the last time.

To make it up to you (as promised) there's no charge.

Sincerely,

BVWS Ticket No. _____   _____

GUARANTEED SERVICE —
— *Our Absolute Commitment*

Source: JWS Technologies & Blue Valley Welding Supply.

ota, have often demonstrated an informal policy of repairing or replacing defective products even if the warranty on them has recently expired. Marriott Hotels has also proved willing to compensate inconvenienced customers when the inconvenience falls just outside the coverage stipulated by its various guarantees; it promises fifteen-minute room service, for example, but doesn't often quibble with a customer's perception of late or failed service, even when the delivery was made just under the time limit. Friendly's, on the other hand, once offered a guarantee that promised a free sundae if lunch wasn't served to a customer within five minutes. But some of the restaurants denied compensation during especially busy lunch periods, claiming that the guarantee wasn't in force at those times—those times when customers have the most to gain from such a guarantee.

It is also important to consider the question of how guarantee compensation, once it has been approved, is to find its way into the customer's hands. Time is critical; the idea is to restore the customer's faith in the company before he or she has a chance to develop an ingrained resentment or to move to a competitor. Notifying a customer that he or she is due compensation is half the battle, but if the actual payment is delayed the customer could rightfully become skeptical. One executive who arrived at an upscale New York hotel was told that no rooms were available despite the fact that his reservation was on record. The front desk was extremely apologetic, set him up at a neighboring hotel, and told him that their policy was to provide him with a coupon for a free suite on his next visit; the coupon, they said, would be sent by mail. As the weeks passed and no coupon arrived, the executive became irritated all over again with the hotel. The coupon never arrived, and the executive never stayed at that hotel again. Despite having in place a powerful implicit guarantee that was appropriately triggered by the staff, the failure to provide a mechanism for promptly delivering a promised payout sabotaged the hotel's efforts to retain a customer.

Besides ensuring that guarantees can be easily triggered and quickly paid out on, companies also need to set up the means for recording, organizing, distributing, and reviewing information about guarantee triggerings and payouts. Retaining customer loyalty is only part of the benefit of a guarantee; an even bigger payoff is learning about quality problems and having an opportunity to fix them. But this payoff occurs only if a company rigorously tracks who is triggering guarantees and for what reasons and then places the information—in a form that allows spotting key problem areas and trends—in the hands of managers who are in a position to do something about it. We'll examine this process in detail in the next chapter, but for now suffice it to say that if a company's guarantee data are allowed to slip between the cracks, that company will experience the pain of payouts without profiting from them.

Many companies—particularly those in manufacturing—will have to take care to extend their guarantee mechanisms to dealers, distributors, repair services, and other third parties who directly interact with customers on behalf of the company. In some cases, ensuring that the guarantee is being appropriately implemented will require tightening the links between the company and the third parties, so that the company has more say about how the third party operates; otherwise, even the best-intentioned guarantee could evaporate in the hands of third-party service representatives who have no stake whatsoever in the program. Companies in this position must take special pains to monitor end-customer satisfaction with the guarantee program in order to make sure that the program is being delivered as intended.

Special Considerations for Complex Services

Guarantee triggering presents special concerns and opportunities for professional service firms and other companies offering complex, relatively high-cost services or products, such as catering businesses or manufacturers of large computer systems. Because these businesses tend to be heavily invested in a relatively small number of clients, they usually can't afford to learn through a torrent of guarantee payouts. For some of these companies, even a single triggering can be financially devastating. These issues require setting up mechanisms that allow for customizing the details of the guarantee process to each customer's situation.

Identification of individual customer needs is absolutely essential for these companies. The onus is clearly on the service or product provider to develop as comprehensive a list as possible of requirements and objectives and to manage customers' expectations by negotiating clear and concise specifications of the service or product to be delivered for each element of the project. One sales training organization that offers a full money-back satisfaction guarantee, for example, has worked with clients to develop detailed lists of critical success factors for each stage of the training process. Thus the firm and its clients might agree ahead of time that instructor charisma is critical to success in the classroom, while providing individual feedback to trainees is critical to on-the-job training. It's no wonder the company is so careful: The average customer accounts for about 10 percent of its annual revenues.

During the process of needs specification, a company should strive to obtain a degree of "reasonableness" from the customer and to establish a level of expectations that it can actually achieve. Performance objectives should be clearly defined and as specific as possible. They should be measurable, with a preestablished objective or subjective yardstick for determining whether or not objectives have been met: Does the communications network support the specified number of simultaneous phone conversations and computer data transfers? Has the health care plan reduced customer costs by 5 percent? Have the management consulting services helped the client achieve a competitive edge? Performance objectives should also establish responsibilities, both for the customer's and the product or service provider's employees. If the product or service ultimately meets the specified objectives, a reasonable customer will hesitate before triggering the guarantee even if there is another source of dissatisfaction. At a minimum, the customer is unlikely to feel cheated, misled, or deceived.

All this is more easily said than done. Developing a thorough list of terms, obligations, and conditions to cover a complex relationship can be time-consuming and may still not cover every contingency. Customers, too, can easily tire of the effort required at their end to develop an absolutely thorough definition of objectives, obligations, and feedback mechanisms. Still, a lack of persistence in pursuing these goals can be disastrous to some companies offering a powerful guarantee.

It is also worth noting that developing even the most exhaustive set of requirements and specifications may do little good if the people providing the information from the customer side are not representative of, or do not see eye to eye with, all of the client employees and managers who will be involved in the project. One consulting firm had this experience with a large-scale provider of technology services. The customer continued to express dissatisfaction with the consultants' efforts no matter how assiduously the firm worked to meet the agreed-upon specifications. Finally, the consultants discovered that the customer manager who had brought them in on the project was thoroughly disliked by most other managers at the company, essentially dooming to failure any efforts made to his specifications. The consulting firm now makes a point of performing the needs evaluation process with a wider group of client representatives.

Another special consideration is that of tracking and monitoring performance. A complex services firm that waits until the end of a project to find out if a customer is dissatisfied will not be in a position to do anything about it. Such companies need to develop quality-assurance programs to continually monitor their performance customer by customer and to alert team members to deviations so that they can act to correct them before they get out of control. They must establish measurement systems for routine checks on performance and create a regular feedback loop with the customer and within the firm to facilitate organizational learning.

During each phase of the project or on some regular basis, written and verbal feedback should be obtained from those within the customer's organization charged with evaluating the program's progress. At the provider's urging, the customer may want to select a cross section of frontline employees, managers, and project administrators to form a quality-assurance committee to assess progress. Control groups may also be required for statistical validation. Formal mechanisms for disseminating error data throughout the company as the project unfolds will help refine team members' understanding of the customer's needs and ensure that the same mistakes are not committed repeatedly.

Some companies will want to set up a process for specifying ahead of time who will have the right to pull the trigger on a guarantee. This is a nonissue for products or services sold to consumers, or for businesses where a single manager—the purchasing manager, say, or even the CEO—clearly is responsible for assessing the quality of the service or product. But providers of complex services and products to organizations will sometimes be dealing with several managers, who are perhaps scattered across more than one department or even division. Which customer manager will measure satisfaction and decide whether the conditions of the guarantee have or have not been met? In general, the individual or individuals who authorize funding for the product or service can be expected to have the final decision on whether the guarantee has been satisfied. However, operating personnel directly involved with the project may be in a better position to pass judgment. Their input could be essential for a fair performance evaluation.

One information services firm authorized only the top-level manager of one of its clients to file complaints. This executive was not involved in operations, however, and did not want to take time to evaluate the firm's performance; he never even distributed the firm's complaint forms to the operating personnel. The operating personnel were aware of problems with the service, but didn't feel they had the authority to complain, and were hesitant to tell their supervisors that they were having problems they couldn't solve themselves. Thus representatives of the information services firm weren't learning about the problems and were deprived of an opportunity to correct them. The problems continued to mount until even the oblivious executive couldn't fail to recognize them. By this time the situation was out of control and the client terminated the provider's contract. In contrast, the sales training organization mentioned earlier specifies that a cross section of client employees ranging from frontline operators to executive decision makers jointly make any decisions about invoking the guarantee; this company rarely lets client problems get out of hand.

Preparing the Front Lines

Any organization hoping to do well with an extraordinary guarantee must inculcate a vision of customer satisfaction in every employee, from the executives down to frontline operating personnel. If employees don't develop a sense of urgency about meeting customers' needs through the guarantee, the company would be better off without it.

How can a company ensure that its employees buy into the guarantee program, that they understand what their role is in making it work? The answer is extensive communication: Management must enlist every means at its disposal to articulate the goals of the guarantee program in a manner that transmits management's own enthusiasm and that makes it clear that all employees play a major role in meeting an exceptional, difficult, and important challenge.

There are any number of ways to get the idea across to employees. Weyerhaeuser put out a monthly newsletter to employees called *Customer Satisfaction*, in which it regularly talked up its guarantee program. The Union National Bank in Manhattan, Kansas, had all employees one day a week wear red T-shirts emblazoned with "OOPS," the name of its guarantee program.

JWS Technologies introduced its guarantee to employees through the following letter from the president:

Dear _____ :

I am writing to you to introduce an exciting new adventure that our company will be embarking on. But first, I need to give you some background information.

You are probably aware that the industrial gas business is highly competitive and becomes increasingly more competitive each year. This is a result of several factors; more producers are buying/starting distributors, existing dealers are opening new branches, and many customers think of our products as commodities, like gasoline. Additionally, all the service is about the same—our service is really no better or worse than any of our competitors. As a result, price has become the important issue.

I have concluded from the above that in order to maintain our survival and growth, we need to differentiate ourselves from our competitors. We have to look, smell, taste, and BE much better than our competitors. Frank Perdue did it with chickens, Vlasic did it with pickles, Federal Express did it with mail service, Domino's did it with pizza. They did it with the total support of all employees, and a dedication to OUTSTANDING SERVICE.

The letter goes on to describe the guarantee and the role employees will play in its implementation. It may seem like a drawn-out way to get the idea across, but putting the guarantee into the context of the company's broad concerns and strategies can help employees to see the guarantee as more than just another promotion.

Whenever possible, written communications should be supplemented by face-to-face meetings between managers and employees, allowing for discussion of the ideas behind the guarantee program and the changes it will engender in people's jobs. Meetings could be as simple as a single, brief meeting to discuss the content of the guarantee and the mechanisms for making good on it; or they could entail several formal training sessions, as was the case at Xerox when it wanted to ensure that its field and customer service personnel were prepared to cope with all the implications of its guarantee from both a technical and a customer satisfaction point of view.

When meeting with employees to introduce a guarantee program, managers should strive to create an open and non-confrontational atmosphere: All employees should feel that they are being encouraged to participate and that their suggestions or concerns will be listened to and, if appropriate, acted on.

Hotel chain Hampton Inn was particularly successful in winning over employees to its guarantee through a series of well-planned meetings. Managers started out not by throwing the guarantee at employees, but rather by leading them along the line of reasoning that led to the guarantee. Employees were asked questions such as: "If you were a guest, what problems might limit your satisfaction?" "What are the touches that would result in your being 100 percent satisfied?" Employees were encouraged to identify with customers coping with everything from brusk reservation clerks to parking lots with burned out bulbs to rooms with noisy air conditioning systems. They examined complaint letters. They discussed the ramifications of a dissatisfied customer: The average guest stays at a Hampton Inn twelve nights a year, and many travelers base their decision about what hotel to select on recommendations from friends and associates. "What would YOU do if you were treated poorly at a hotel?" employees were asked.

Employees were next asked to consider how an unconditional guarantee of satisfaction might help. To confirm their guesses, they were shown videotapes of guests reacting to the news that their dissatisfaction entitled them to having the cost of the night's stay waived. And to allow them to prepare for other possible customer reactions to the guarantee, the employees were given a list of frequently asked questions about guarantees.

By the time the meetings were over, few Hampton Inn employees doubted the importance of the guarantee program or of their role in it. This buy-in was emphasized some months after the rollout of the program when a hotel industry magazine ran a letter criticizing the Hampton Inn guarantee program as impossible to maintain. The magazine promptly received an answering letter from a desk clerk at a California Hampton Inn, who, acting entirely on his own, wrote: "I quite enjoy bragging about where I work. If you have an excellent product, you should have enough intestinal fortitude to stand behind it." How many companies can count on that sort of support from their frontline employees?

An organization need not hold meetings as extensive and carefully planned as Hampton Inn's to get the message through to its employees. Quimobasicos held three relatively short meetings to introduce its guarantee to employees. But it achieved maximum benefit from the events by focusing on an employee "leverage point"—an issue of extreme importance to employees that could be related to the guarantee effort. In the case of Quimobasicos, employees were concerned about how the company was going to fare in the face of increased competition from U.S. companies as the United States and Mexico reached free trade agreements; many employees feared that the company would lose customers and start laying people off. When the chemical company's managers discussed the guarantee program, they emphasized that the guarantee would be crucial in reinforcing customer loyalty, and maintained that this loyalty would be the company's greatest weapon in fending off challenges from north of the border. As a result, employees were instantly invested in the program and determined to make the guarantee work.

The Power of Empowerment

Although organizational structure is gradually evolving, most companies still operate on the hierarchical, near-militaristic model established centuries ago. In this scheme, frontline employees are tightly limited as to the actions they can take; to do something that is outside the bounds of their well-defined jobs, they first have to ask permission of a manager. This setup worked well a hundred or even thirty years ago when the greatest challenge to businesses was turning out as much product as possible at the lowest possible cost. But now that businesses are fighting tooth and nail to win the loyalty of the most fractured, finicky, and sophisticated population of buyers the world has ever known, rigid hierarchy has become a straightjacket that chokes off the very kinds of actions that are most needed to satisfy customers. Ironically, even the military has long since abandoned strict hierarchy, placing a far greater premium on the initiative of platoon leaders than on their blind obedience to generals.

An extraordinary guarantee probably won't work if employees aren't empowered to do what it takes to satisfy customers. That means giving employees the right, even the obligation, to make operating decisions, to spend company money, and, in almost every way, to be prepared to go above and beyond to make things right. Given the level of complexity of today's products and services, there is simply no way that managers can anticipate most of the problems that will crop up, let alone specify processes for fixing all of them. Increasingly, managers must instead give employees the tools and authority they need to fix problems as they arise.

In the context of a guarantee program, the empowerment of employees must begin with the establishment of an environment of blameless error. The point of the guarantee, it must be emphasized to employees, is not to determine which employees screwed up so that they can be punished, but rather to determine which processes are faulty so that they can be patched up. In such an environment, employees will look at error identification as an act to be rewarded rather than as an act of corporate self-immolation. It is up to managers to prove as much to employees through their actions. Unfortunately, U.S. companies have so far not been world leaders in this endeavor. An Ernst & Young/American Quality Foundation study found that U.S. automakers involve only 28 percent of their workers in employee suggestion programs, compared with 78 percent of Japanese autoworkers so involved. And 60 percent of German computer manufacturers incorporate customer complaints in the new product design process, compared with only 26 percent in the United States.

There is no shortage of examples to demonstrate the effectiveness of empowerment. It is well known, for example, that Japanese car factory assembly lines can be brought to a screeching halt by any employee anywhere along the way who sees an error creeping through. For decades, managers at U.S. auto manufacturers cringed at the idea of giving thousands of employees the power to stop car production, incurring losses of tens of thousands of dollars, just to fix a few loose bolts or faulty electrical connections. Today, however, faced with the loss of billions of dollars in market share to Japanese competitors, U.S. automakers have begun to set up the same sorts of stop-production switches along their own assembly lines. American companies have learned the hard way that these problems *must* be addressed on the spot by the people who are closest to them, lest they slip through the cracks and torpedo quality. The same, of course, is true at service companies. Nordstrom's employee handbook is one page long and contains eight sentences. Among them: "Rule No. 1: Use good judgment in all situations. There will be no additional rules."

This is not to say that companies ought to throw out their employee manuals. Managers can provide employees with more authority in specific areas that are critical to the guarantee program or to certain elements of customer satisfaction. That's what Montgomery Ward did when it changed a long-standing policy of requiring a supervisor's okay to accept a return and instead invested its 7,700 sales clerks with that authority. Similarly, American Airlines gave its flight attendants and passenger service personnel the power to compensate inconvenienced passengers with several hundred dollars worth of cash, credit, or tickets. In addition to saving customers the irritation of having to wait for supervisor approval, such authorization allows employees to feel more directly responsible for customer satisfaction. Both the customer and the employee are gratified by the resulting speedy resolution of difficulties.

Besides addressing key components of customer satisfaction, such selective empowerment serves as a means of letting management get its feet wet with empowerment. Managers soon discover that rather than breaking the company with extravagantly poor judgment, empowered employees generally rise to the occasion with good judgment. This is especially true in the charged environment of an extraordinary guarantee program. One small example: After Marriott hotels rolled out a new guarantee program, employees were authorized to implement any satisfaction-enhancing routines they could think of. Managers of some of the hotels were soon puzzled to hear that guests were showing up at the front desk and demanding to know where the pancakes were. As it turned out, staff members of one hotel had taken it on themselves to set up a portable griddle in the middle of the lobby each morning to cook pancakes to order for passing guests. This amenity had such a positive impact on guests that they sought it out at other Marriotts, and corporate management considered making it a standard feature.

Making Guarantees Pay Off for Employees

Just as a comprehensive quality improvement program should incorporate some mechanism for tying employee compensation to quality successes, so a guarantee program should financially reward employees for the success of the guarantee. Senior managers have a built-in incentive for making the guarantee work: The corporate bottom line will rise and fall with the program's success or failure. Employees should be similarly invested.

The compensation plan need not be complicated. JWS set up a modest guarantee-linked inducement for its employees in the form of a "cookie-jar": an account into which the company placed four dollars per employee for every day the company operated without a delivery error. The plan was specifically tied to performance under the guarantee; the money employees took home from the fund—up to $1,000 a year—was in addition to previously established bonuses and profit-sharing plans.

Nor do incentives have to take the form of cash. Oakley Millwork offered all its employees a free trip to Hawaii for two if they could keep the company free of backorders for a year; as a reminder, the company kept a Hawaiian travel poster and a calendar on the lunchroom wall. The employees went seven months without a backorder before finally stumbling—but management provided a company cruise as a consolation prize.

When paying staff bonuses for guarantee program performance, companies should take care to focus the incentives on receiving and resolving customer complaints and on fixing the sources of complaints rather than on simply reducing the number of complaints. Emphasizing low numbers of complaints could inadvertently cause employees to discourage or even ignore complaints. Some managers might even encourage the suppression of guarantee triggerings to reduce payouts and thus obtain a short-term boost in profits. Needless to say, such actions defeat the purpose of an extraordinary guarantee program.

Getting the Message to Customers

It's finally time to tell customers about the guarantee. That comprises two tasks: determining how the guarantee will be phrased, and determining how it will be presented to customers. One obvious goal of the rollout is to invest the guarantee with maximum marketing impact, so that customers will be more likely to do business with the company either because the guarantee increases their faith in the product or because the guarantee gives the company an aura of quality and dependability. The guarantee presentation should also address a more subtle but potentially more important goal: ensuring that customers remain aware of the guarantee after their initial commitment, so that they will trigger it if dissatisfied. In addition to providing the most effective means of identifying quality leaks, guarantee triggerings are a company's best hope of hanging on to that 60 percent of all consumers who tend to switch brands or companies rather than complain.

Wording the Guarantee

An extraordinary guarantee should be stated in clear, concise language. Although the guarantee is, in effect, a legally binding contract, it should not read like a legal document. It should not attempt to provide for every possible contingency. It should not be diluted by a sea of fine print. It should not sound like a thinly disguised advertisement, filled with hyperbole and promotional language intended to manipulate the customer. Instead, it should quickly and effectively communicate the company's willingness to stand behind its product and service and to take care of the customer.

The guarantee is a promise made by the company to a customer, and it should have the strong, clear, uncompromising tone of a promise. Remember L. L. Bean's guarantee?

> Everything we sell is backed by a 100% unconditional guarantee. We do not want you to have anything from L. L. Bean that is not completely satisfactory. Return anything you buy from us at any time for any reason it proves otherwise.

Kelly Services (the providers of "Kelly Girl" office temps) also employs a confident, straightforward tone in its guarantee:

> This will certify that all services provided by Kelly Services, Inc., are unconditionally guaranteed to be performed in an acceptable, workmanlike manner, and that each Kelly employee is fully qualified to serve in the capacity specified by the Customer. Upon reasonable notice from a Customer, all charges for unsatisfactory service will be canceled.

The no-nonsense phrasing here projects the very sense of professionalism and uncompromising reliability that the company wants customers to associate with its services. It is also worth noting that the guarantee is always signed by the company's chairman, its president, and the local manager.

A guarantee need not be unconditional to benefit from strong phrasing. In some cases, focusing the guarantee on key service or product elements can add impact. Here, for example, is the guarantee offered by the Minneapolis Marriott:

> Our quality commitment to you is to provide:
>
> - A friendly, efficient check-in
> - A clean, comfortable room, where everything works
> - A friendly, efficient check-out
>
> If we, in YOUR opinion, do not deliver on this

commitment, we will give you $20.00 in cash. No questions asked. It is your interpretation.

We want to do our job right the first time and exceed your expectations.

This guarantee hits the major hot buttons for hotel guests—friendliness, efficiency, cleanliness, and comfort—and emphasizes the fact that the customer gets to call the shots when it comes to quality. It does a good job of suggesting the idea that this is essentially an unconditional guarantee, although it is nominally limited to certain important service issues.

Delta Dental Plan, a Massachusetts provider of dental care insurance, also lists the specific performance elements it guarantees. In Delta's case, there are seven elements, each carrying a specific payout. Combining seven separate guarantee points might normally result in an overly long, cumbersome guarantee statement. But Delta found a way to organize and highlight the seven points so that the overall impression is clear and forceful:

Delta Dental Plan's Seven Guarantees

Problem Solving
Resolution of a problem or initial status update within one business day.
Refund: $50 for each service failure

Cost Containment
Total cost of all paid claims during a policy year at least 10% less than the total value of the dentists' usual stated fees.
Refund: Refund or credit equal to the dollar difference

Subscriber I.D. Cards
Complete and accurate subscriber identification cards received within 15 calendar days upon receipt of complete and accurate enrollment forms.
Refund: $25 refund or credit for EACH late or inaccurate card

Claims Processing
Over the course of a policy year, at least 85% of all
claims processed within 15 calendar days upon receipt of complete and accurate claim form.
  Refund: Refund or credit of a full month's administration fee

Smooth Conversion
A smooth conversion process or smooth implementation (for companies without previous dental insurance).
  Refund: Refund or credit of a full month's administration fee

Balance Billing
Acceptance by participating Massachusetts dentists
of Delta Dental Plan's contract allowance as payment
in full; no billing patients for the remainder.
  Refund: $50 refund for each occurrence

Management Reports
Upon request, four standard monthly reports mailed
to the company in one package within ten calendar
days following the end of each month.
  Refund: $50 refund or credit per package

A customer or potential customer looking over this statement
can tell at a glance what basic service elements Delta is addressing through its guarantee, and how it intends to make good on
these promises. The very specific description of the refunds
also suggests that there will be little argument when it comes
to triggering the guarantee.
    Although restrictions and limitations tend to weaken guar-
antees, they are sometimes necessary. If reasonably well-inte-
grated into the statement, they won't substantially detract from
it. AT&T Computer Systems' guarantee remained a strong-
sounding one, for example, despite the restrictions:

Customer Satisfaction Guarantee

AT&T Computer Systems is committed to customer satisfaction. Your satisfaction is the highest standard of quality upon which we measure ourselves and we are pleased to extend to you the following guarantee: If you are not fully satisfied and delighted with the AT&T Computer Systems product or service support furnished to you, as new, by AT&T Computer Systems or its participating Authorized Reseller, just call 1 (800) 344-3444 within 60 days of delivery if you do the installation, or within 60 days of installation by AT&T or its participating Authorized Reseller. If the problem cannot be resolved, your money will be promptly refunded when the products are returned in the condition received.

This money-back guarantee is not in place of the AT&T Limited Warranty and Limitation of Liability. This guarantee excludes the following: wiring, products and services covered by third-party financing, custom software, and non-AT&T logo products.

Note that the guarantee says that customers should not only be satisfied but "delighted" with the product. Note also the inclusion of a telephone number, which provides customers with a clear and accessible means of triggering the guarantee—and the company with a good chance of winning back an irritated customer.

Restrictions and limitations in guarantees can actually enhance customer satisfaction if they serve to better align customer expectations with reasonable levels of performance. GTE decided to offer an unconditional guarantee with its Airfone in-flight telephone service. But a straightforward guarantee might have misled some customers into believing that the company was promising to provide clear, dependable service; in fact, owing to technical and regulatory hurdles, the service sometimes resulted in garbled, inaudible, or interrupted conversations. GTE, however, was willing to make good on these bad calls. Here is how GTE confronted the situation in its guarantee, which was printed below the instructions for using the phone:

> CUSTOMER SATISFACTION GUARANTEE: We stand behind the quality of our service. However, due to the nature of radio wave transmission, there may be times communication is impaired due to events such as adverse weather conditions or changes in terrain. If at any time you are dissatisfied with your Airfone call, dial "0" while in flight for GTE Airfone Customer Service. After you reach your destination, dial 1-800 AIRFONE (1-800-247-3663).

Note that GTE was offering to accept guarantee triggerings on the spot—that is, on the plane, via phone—but also had the foresight to provide a land number, since a customer could hardly use the Airfone to trigger the guarantee if the phone wasn't working.

Words generally carry meanings beyond the obvious ones, and some companies might want to take advantage of this principle. Lawnmower manufacturer Toro, for example, wrote up its guarantee—which promised that its mowers would start right up—with the aid of a firm that specializes in analyzing the emotional content of sentences; the goal was to communicate as much emotion as possible, since buying decisions are considered by many experts to be based largely on feelings rather than practical reasoning. For what it's worth, Toro's sales in the first two years after introduction of the guarantee rose 30 percent and 50 percent, respectively.

Presenting the Guarantee

Some companies might want to print up the guarantee statement by itself, and then stick it in the box with the product or post it up on the wall of the service establishment. But others will want to take the opportunity to put the guarantee into some larger context, that is, to frame it with some sort of additional text that could serve to enhance the impact of or clarify certain issues regarding the guarantee.

Clothing retailer Lands' End, for example, chose to call attention to the unconditional nature of its guarantee with a few sentences that also serve to add some drama and a touch of humor:

> The world is full of guarantees, no two alike. As a rule, the more words they contain, the more their protection is limited. The Lands' End guarantee has always been an unconditional one. It reads:
>
> > "If you are not completely satisfied with any item you buy from us, at any time during your use of it, return it and we will refund your full purchase price."
>
> We mean every word of it. Whatever. Whenever. Always. But to make sure this is perfectly clear, we've decided to simplify it further.
>
> GUARANTEED. Period.

A guarantee statement can also be accompanied by useful information related to the guarantee, such as how a customer can go about getting the company to address the problem or how to trigger the guarantee. That's what Holiday Inn did with its guarantee, which was printed on cards placed in the rooms. The card listed three separate means guests could use to get the company to make good on the guarantee: They could contact the manager or the front desk, or they could dial an 800 number that would put them in touch with a corporate customer service representative.

If done carefully, a company can pack quite a bit of information into its guarantee presentation without diluting the guarantee's impact. First Image, the computer microfilm producers, offered an extremely straighforward guarantee, but chose to precede it with an introduction:

Service Guarantee

Our Philosophy
   [Our] service philosophy can be summed up in three points:

1. There is no room for mediocrity
2. You should never pay for anything less than pre-mium service.
3. The customer is the best judge of quality.

This philosophy is more than just a credo; it dictates how we work. And to demonstrate just how serious we are, we give you an unconditional service guarantee.

Our Guarantee
Our main objective is to satisfy you. That's why we've designed a service guarantee that is uncondi-tional, easy to use, and covers every single aspect of our service. What this means is if you're not satisfied with a job—for any reason—you are entitled to cancel up to 100% of the charges for that job. No if's, and's or but's.

It's long—but First Image isn't nearly through yet. Because of the complexity of its service, the company required customers to go through a number of simple steps when triggering the guarantee, including filling out a claim form. Rather than tucking away the requirements in fine print, or springing them on customers when they called to complain, First Image de-cided to spell out the steps right there in the guarantee, preempting concerns about delays, confusion, or confrontation that many customers have when they consider triggering a guarantee. In addition, the explanation gave the company a chance to reemphasize its commitment to confronting any sources of customer dissatisfaction and correcting them. Here, for example, is the third of the six steps described on the form:

One of the most important parts of the claim form is the percentage of the job charges you'd like canceled. This is your opportunity to let us know just how dissatisfied you are. If you are completely dissatisfied with our service, write in 100%. If you are only partially dissatisfied, write in 68%, 20%, 5%—what-ever matches your level of dissatisfaction.

It's simple, it communicates trust, and it helps the customer feel comfortable with what might otherwise be an awkward triggering process (see Figure 8-2).

One effective way to introduce a guarantee to customers is to write them a letter describing the nature of the guarantee program, the thinking behind it, and the impact it would have on them. Since letters by nature tend to be more informal and longer than brochures or certificates, they give a company a chance to discuss the guarantee at greater length and to take a more personal tack.

Delta Dental, for example, introduced its guarantee to customers and prospective customers via letter. The company also took the occasion to explain what the guarantee would *not* do. In bouncing the guarantee off several customers before rolling it out, Delta had learned that some customers might assume that the cost of maintaining a guarantee program would result in a price increase—and it knew customers weren't willing to pay extra for the guarantee. In addition, some large customers were already receiving levels of service that were, on average, above the levels promised in the new guarantee; these customers might wonder if the guarantee meant that Delta was no longer committed to providing them with this superior level of service.

In its letters, Delta assured customers that there would be no cost increase associated with the guarantee plan, and that customers could expect to receive at *least* the level of service they had been receiving before the guarantee; most could expect even better service. Delta brought home this message in more detail by way of personal meetings with most clients. It also launched a preemptive strike against competitors who might try to match its guarantee with selected accounts. The company pointed out that its guarantee was merely the most visible element of a comprehensive effort to enhance its quality and efficiency. But a competitor that offered a guarantee to just a few clients wasn't going to change the way it did business; it would just throw more people at selected accounts. *That*, noted Delta, was how a company let its costs get out of control.

Manufacturers can of course call attention to their guarantees right on the product's packaging. Both Prestone and Kiwi

Figure 8-2. First Image lets *customers* decide how much they should be compensated.

Source: Courtesy of First Image.

shoe polish pushed their strong guarantees with small pull-off tabs attached to the products that trumpeted on the front "$100 Radiator Guarantee" and "Money-Back Guarantee," respectively, with the details in small print on the other side. Nonprofessional service companies can accomplish much the same thing with posters and counter cards. McDonald's, for example, plastered colorful presentations of its guarantees on wall and ceiling-hung displays, cards, and place mats.

Although it may be taking things to extremes, some companies have gone so far as to incorporate their guarantees into the product's name. Macklanburg-Duncan's "35-year" silicone caulking is guaranteed for—what else?—thirty-five years. (It should be noted that Macklanburg-Duncan's enthusiasm for the guarantee did not extend to a generous or convenient refund policy: The company requires the return of the empty tube and a purchase receipt—items not normally retained for thirty-five years—before refunding the cost of the tube.) Service companies too can indulge in this odd form of guarantee promotion. One public relations firm actually named itself after its guarantee: Results Only Communications, Inc., which charges its clients not strictly by the hour, as most PR firms do, but according to how much press it gets them. As the company's name suggests, no results, no fees.

Advertising the Guarantee

Anyone who doubts the power of advertising should consider the Federal Express campaign that declared, "When it absolutely, positively has to be there overnight." To this day, many people think that slogan continues to embody Federal Express's guarantee to deliver packages by mid-morning the next day. But that campaign ended in the early 1980s, at a time when the company did not guarantee morning delivery. If a decade-old advertisement can conjure up associations with a powerful guarantee that didn't even exist then, imagine what a brand-new campaign based on a real guarantee can accomplish.

Xerox put together a tour de force of advertising and marketing materials based on its new guarantee for copiers, all of it designed to emphasize the guarantee's broad, unconditional protection. One ad is headlined, "Finally, a guarantee that lets you decide if you're satisfied"; in it, a cartoon character is angrily throwing away sheets of paper, saying, "Guarantees! Everybody's got one, and they're all the same. Loopholes and legal blather. They talk about satisfaction, but after you sift through all the fine print, it seems like *they're* tellin' *me* if I'm satisfied or not." The copy goes on to stress the guarantee's simplicity and to make the connection between the guarantee and the company's confidence in its equipment and its dedication to customer satisfaction.

Other Xerox ads and marketing materials are more subtle, but no less effective, in highlighting the superiority of the company's guarantee over competitors' guarantees. One brochure, for example, quotes an independent publication that performs copier evaluations as calling the guarantee "unprecedented" and "a display of confidence." And a Xerox booklet that is designed to sound like an objective guide to purchasing a copier includes a section on warranties that warns buyers to carefully consider warranty limitations; the booklet doesn't mention Xerox's warranty, but it's clear which brand of copier will benefit from the advice.

AT&T long-distance phone services, widely recognized as one of the most sophisticated advertisers in the world, has also used ads to underscore the strength of its guarantee. One ad places a photo of an AT&T-affiliated pay phone next to a photo of a Concorde jet, with the headline, "Both come with a service guarantee. One travels faster." (See Figure 8-3.) The text notes that the call is faster, and states that "no matter where you call from, you're guaranteed AT&T's low prices, efficient operators, immediate credit for misdialed calls, and the ability to call anywhere in the world."

Dozens of other companies have headlined extraordinary guarantees in ad campaigns, including Nissan (see Figure 8-4), Delta Hotels and Resorts, Quaker State Motor Oil, Olympus cameras, and Florsheim shoes. Nor does a company need a multimillion-dollar ad budget to flaunt its guarantee in print. Oakley Millwork and Casavant Frères organs are examples of

Figure 8-3. AT&T's service guarantee adds credibility to the claim.

Both come with a service guarantee. One travels faster.

A supersonic Concorde can travel up to 1,367 miles per hour. But it only flies to London and Paris three times a day.

Calls made on the AT&T Worldwide Intelligent Network can travel up to 186,000 miles per second. AT&T reaches over 250 countries and locations, 24 hours a day, 365 days a year.

No long distance carrier can connect you faster. No carrier reaches more destinations. In fact, AT&T is the most reliable long distance company you can choose. And, when you do, you get a service guarantee.

That means no matter where you call from, you're guaranteed AT&T's low prices, efficient operators, immediate credit for misdialed calls, and the ability to call anywhere in the world. So, when you're on the road, now more than ever, it pays to choose AT&T.

If you want a service guarantee, make sure you hear "Thank you for using AT&T." There's no way to make your connections faster. We're here to help. For assistance, call 1 800 222-0300.

AT&T
The right choice.

Source: (Copyright) 1989 AT&T.

Figure 8-4. The Nissan Satisfaction Commitment™. The most comprehensive full-time customer care program in Canada.

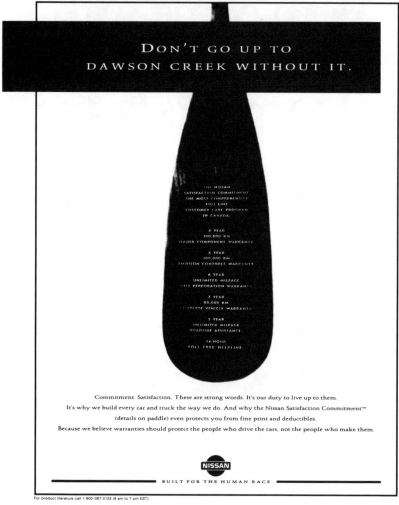

Source: Courtesy of Nissan Canada Inc.

small companies that have made a splash with modest, guar-
antee-oriented print ads that ran in trade publications.

One note of caution: Companies need to make sure that
ad writers don't take too many liberties in pushing the coverage
and simplicity of the guarantee. If the guarantee is truly unconditional, easy to invoke, and likely to make customers feel that
they have been fully compensated for any product or service
failures, then there is little to be concerned about. But if
customers find that there is a gap between the protection
implied by the ad and the reality of the guarantee, the ad may
ultimately do more harm than good.

Selling With the Guarantee

Salespeople are forever looking for ammunition for their
pitches—that is, company or product strengths they can boast
about or competitor weaknesses they can (perhaps subtly) take
jabs at. An extraordinary guarantee can be a rocket-powered
grenade if the sales force integrates it properly into its attack.

The makings of a good sales pitch, of course, vary with
the company, the salesperson, and the customer. In general,
however, here are some ways to make use of the guarantee
when selling:

- *Promise breakthrough service, then guarantee it*. Instead of
leading off with the guarantee, it is often more effective to put
it in the context of what the customer is really looking for—
which is better service or product, not compensation for disappointment. By emphasizing the quality of the product or
service first, and then declaring that the company stands
behind this promise of quality with a powerful guarantee, you
are more likely to get the customer to see the guarantee as
reinforcing the key message.

- *Underscore commitment to the guarantee*. Many companies
offer a guarantee, and some customers may have fallen into the
habit of tuning them out. It probably bears stressing more than
once that the company has gone through great pains to come
up with a guarantee that is truly exceptional, and that everyone
from the chairman of the board to the people who answer the

phones is dedicated to making it work for the customer. Make sure that all the strong elements of the guarantee—the ease of triggering, the lack of restrictions, the generosity and speed of the payout—are pointed out. The message can be further emphasized by presenting a written copy of the guarantee, preferably over the personal signatures of one or more senior executives as well as any managers who are specifically involved in this account.

- *Discuss the link to quality.* Most managers do not immediately recognize that an extraordinary guarantee requires a concomitant boost in quality and sometimes even a drastic revamping of the organization. In addition to explaining how this is true for your company, you can drive the point home by asking the customer to imagine what his or her own company would have to do before it would feel comfortable offering an extraordinary guarantee.

- *Stress partnership.* A powerful guarantee ensures that customer dissatisfaction will immediately be translated into pain for the service or product provider. Thus you can rightly point out that your company and the customer's company will be in the same boat: The customer's goals become the provider's goals, and the customer's problems are the provider's problems. Many customers will prefer—and should prefer—to think in terms of a partnership rather than a buyer/seller relationship.

- *Call attention to competitors' guarantees.* Some salespeople might feel safe directly comparing their companies' guarantees to the weaker guarantees of competitors. In many businesses, however, it is considered unprofessional to directly disparage competitors. A more subtle way to make the point is to urge the customer to examine other guarantees and even to consider making an extraordinary guarantee a prerequisite for all its vendors. Customers might even consider writing the guarantee into their bid requirements.

Playing up a guarantee in any form could be inappropriate for some professional service firms; if presented prominently, a guarantee could seem tacky, unprofessional, and even unethical (we'll discuss guarantee ethics in more detail in a later chapter). For the great majority of professional service firms, however, a more low-key incorporation of an extraordinary guarantee into a sales pitch is not likely to cause problems, and could help. Some consultancies, for example, place the guarantee statement near the end of their proposals. Similarly, in meetings with potential clients, the guarantee can be mentioned as a kicker, or even in a "by-the-way" fashion. If handled skillfully, such subtlety can magnify the impact of the guarantee.

Testing the Waters

If a company is embarking on an extraordinary guarantee with its eyes open, it will wisely recognize that rolling out the program always requires a certain leap of faith. After all, an exceptional guarantee means that a company is putting its reputation, as well as its profitability, on the line, with little margin for error. No amount of preparation can completely eliminate the risk inherent in such a program.

A company can, however, get some sense of what might be in store for it by going through some limited runs of the program before rolling it out to the entire customer base. McDonald's, for example, tried out its guarantee in selected restaurants before bringing it out nationwide. Similarly, Quimobasicos started by offering its inventory guarantee only to nearby distributors, and even then only for those chemicals for which it had established the best production controls. Both these companies were encouraged by early results and decided to extend their programs. But some companies might be unpleasantly surprised by the results of a limited rollout and opt to withdraw the guarantee before any real damage is done. The sudden yanking of a widely implemented guarantee program, on the other hand, could be embarrassing and costly.

Delta Dental Plan took exceptional pains to ease itself into its guarantee step by step. It first tested out its guarantee on a strictly internal basis by having employees play the role of customers; the company then carefully tracked how often service failures would have led to invoking of the guarantee, and how well its people handled such triggerings. After a few weeks of this simulated rollout, the company enlisted the help of several customers in testing out the guarantee under no-payout conditions. It was only after two months of these limited operations that Delta finally felt comfortable rolling the guarantee out to its full customer base.

It would be an exceptional company, indeed, that found its fully implemented guarantee program going off without a hitch. It is far more likely that a company will find itself facing a raft of unanticipated problems. Fortunately, in most cases, these problems can be turned to the company's advantage. The next chapter discusses some approaches to doing just that.

Chapter 9

Getting the Most Out of the Guarantee

In spite of the attention that zero-defect quality programs received in the 1980s, a company cannot realistically hope to eliminate all sources of error. It can, however, try to minimize errors and mitigate the damage they cause. And therein lies the real benefit of an extraordinary guarantee.

The purpose of an extraordinary guarantee is to bring mistakes to the attention of employees and managers, providing them with the opportunity to win back dissatisfied customers, and to identify and fix those processes that account for a disproportionate share of the company's mistakes. This chapter discusses ways to employ the guarantee to that effect, as well as approaches to enhancing the guarantee and assessing its overall benefit to the company.

The Importance of Error Recovery

A properly implemented extraordinary guarantee will bring people in to complain. Then it is the company's task to make these customers happy. It is a task at which U.S. companies have long fared dismally. In fact, when companies bother to reply to complaints at all—and many don't—they manage to make the customer even more irritated about half the time, according to one business school study. Businesses have paid for this failure, as witnessed by the federal government study that found that 90 percent of disgruntled customers switch loyalties when their complaints are not appropriately addressed, compared with only 54 percent of those customers whose complaints receive a satisfactory response.

Even if only a small percentage of complaints were slipping through the cracks, it would still be too high. As an extreme but telling example, consider the case of a thirty-year customer of a Spokane, Washington, bank who was refused a parking validation by a bank clerk because he hadn't made a deposit that day. The customer complained to the branch manager to no avail, and then took the trouble to drive forty blocks to complain to his regular banker at another branch. The customer warned that if he wasn't called by the end of the day with a satisfactory resolution of the problem, he would withdraw all his money. He didn't get the call, and he pulled his first million out the next morning. The story made national news, and served to remind the embarrassed—and somewhat less well capitalized—bank that it had better start taking customer complaints a little more seriously.

One study of nine hotels in a twenty-one-hotel chain sharply illustrated the botched nature of complaint handling and the subsequent likelihood of negative word of mouth. Of 479 guests who had written letters of complaint to hotel managers over a one-year period, nearly two-thirds had already complained in person at the time of the incident, and a whopping 88 percent of those who had complained reported that hotel employees were unsuccessful in reducing their dissatisfaction.

It is amazing that companies give complaint resolution such short shrift when one considers that it is on average five times as costly to win a new customer as it is to retain an existing one. Automakers can count on bringing in $140,000 over a satisfied buyer's lifetime; appliance makers can expect $2,800 over twenty years; supermarkets get $22,000 from a family over a five-year period. Another way to look at it, according to a study by the U.S. Office of Consumer Affairs, is that every dollar spent on handling complaints brings in anywhere from two dollars to $2.75. Why would a business turn its back on this sort of revenue by ignoring a complaint? Indeed, customers who complain tend to be the most brand-conscious, the most loyal, and the most willing to talk about their experiences with others. How a company responds to their complaints has a greater effect on their loyalty than any other factor.

Companies need to change the mind-set that looks upon complaint handling as a cost rather than as an opportunity. Installing an extraordinary guarantee is clearly a good first step. A good second step is to welcome the resulting complaints, and prepare to stand behind the guarantee.

Going Above and Beyond

Often it does not take a great deal of sacrifice to honor the conditions of a guarantee; typically, the requirements can be satisfied simply by repairing or replacing a product, providing a missing service element (soap in a hotel room, a parking validation in a bank), or returning some or all of a customer's money. Even so, it will at times be tempting to argue with a customer who is manifestly unreasonable in triggering a guarantee. When should a company draw the line?

According to those businesses that have made customer satisfaction an all-encompassing mission, the answer is never. Leonard's Dairy in Norwalk, Connecticut, has literally carved in stone its take on an old adage that sums up such a philosophy. Engraved on a rock outside the store is the message, RULE #1: THE CUSTOMER IS ALWAYS RIGHT. RULE #2: IF THE CUSTOMER IS WRONG, REFER TO RULE NUMBER ONE. It is a simple concept, but not always so simple to execute; after all, just because customers are always right doesn't mean that they're always fair. Lawn care specialist Chemlawn faced this dilemma when a number of its customers claimed after a late frost that the resultant damage to their lawns was owing to bad fertilizer. Rather than arguing, Chemlawn reseeded and replugged the lawns.

Is honoring the guarantee good enough? In many cases, the payout from even a generous guarantee won't completely restore customer satisfaction and faith in the company. Many customers believe, for example, that a repaired appliance is never quite as reliable or functional as it was before the repairs; and a customer kept awake all night in his or her hotel room by a noisy air conditioner won't be any the less tired for getting $40 off the bill.

For these reasons, companies should be prepared to give some customers more than what the guarantee entitles them to. GM's Saturn division recognized that its reputation as a high-quality car manufacturer was at risk when it discovered that some of its cars had been shipped with bad antifreeze that might have corroded some radiators. Under its warranty, Saturn owed the affected owners new radiators. Instead, Saturn gave them brand-new cars—sometimes with extra options—at no additional charge. In this way, the company completely erased any doubts customers might have had about their cars' durability or the company's intention to keep them happy.

Fortunately, paying out beyond the guarantee isn't always as costly as providing a new automobile. Some restaurants instruct servers always to give customers free drinks or dessert when something has gone wrong with the meal—in addition to waiving the cost of the meal. Federal Express's guarantee promises only to refund the shipping costs if it misses a delivery; but the company has sent heavily inconvenienced customers several certificates for free future deliveries.

The management of the Domino's Pizza franchises in the Baltimore area is legendary for its willingness not only to honor its guarantee but to go beyond it. The president personally answers some complaint letters, sometimes including his home phone number and a check for up to ten times the cost of the offending pizza.

For some companies, the desire to keep customers happy is so ingrained that they will stretch to solve customers' problems even when the problem isn't covered by a guarantee and the customer doesn't expect special consideration. Management at the Club Med in Cancun learned that a planeload of guests en route to the resort had been delayed at various airports for hours, twice rerouted, and subjected to rough flying. As the miserable, exhausted, hungry passengers filed into the terminal at 2:00 A.M., they were surprised to find the resort staff waiting for them with snacks and music; furthermore, the staff had talked the guests already at the resort into waiting up and greeting the new arrivals with a party. The new guests' talk of a lawsuit quickly melted into praise for what some later said was the most enjoyable night of their lives. Club Med's thoughtfulness is also good business: The average guest returns three more times, generating a total profit of $2,400. Why not go the extra mile to make sure that unhappy customers don't end up spending most of it somewhere else?

Companies that inculcate in their employees a willingness to go above and beyond what is necessary end up leaving a trail of surprised and grateful customers. One Federal Express sorting clerk pulled out poorly wrapped Christmas gifts, took them home, rewrapped them, and brought them back in time for shipment. A Domino's delivery person, passing by a house that had burned down the night before, saw the family walking around the wreckage; he returned with free pizzas for them. Whenever staff members at the Minneapolis Marriott hear that any of their guests have had a rough day, they send up a "Sweet Dreams" package that includes a cordial, a vase with a carnation, and homemade cookies. A customer at Leonard's Dairy complained when the store ran out of chicken; when a shipment of chicken arrived a half hour later, one of the managers grabbed a package and drove it to the stunned customer's door. Such companies don't have to rely on advertising to convince customers that they really care about them.

Learning From Complaints

Of course, getting good at responding to complaints doesn't mean ignoring the problems that are causing them. While it's true that addressing the needs of disgruntled customers can win their loyalty, a safer and less costly way to earn loyalty is to make sure that fewer customers are disgruntled in the first place.

The complaints generated by an extraordinary guarantee will take care of the first step in the process of plugging quality leaks: identifying the problem areas. The second step—finding a way to limit or even eliminate the problem—can be trickier.

Sometimes a subtle but creative modification in work processes can make all the difference. Bel Canto, a chain of upscale pizza restaurants in New England, was able to cut down significantly on the number of service complaints received by adding one small chore to the servers' duties: If a customer was inadvertently slighted in any way or otherwise suffered any problems, a server posted a note in the kitchen warning that the customer was "at risk" of being dissatisfied. From then on, the customer was to receive special attention. Most of these at-risk customers, basking in the souped-up service, quickly forgot whatever it was that had bothered them and were left with a positive impression of the dining experience.

Another example of how a simple change can make a huge difference in meeting the promise of a guarantee is offered by mail-order garden supplies company Smith & Hawken. The company found that even though it took pains to respond generously to all its customers' complaints, the time taken up by back-and-forth mail correspondence sometimes left customers unimpressed with the results. The solution: The company told employees to settle all gripes on the spot over the phone. Phone bills went way up, but overall costs went down as employees found themselves freed from paperwork. And customers were thoroughly pleased by the prompt action.

A guarantee can make a problem that has always seemed trivial suddenly cry out for fixing. JWS would on rare occasions inadvertently deliver a tank of gas on which the valve didn't work. Standard procedure was simply to get a truck right out to the customer to swap the tank for a functioning one. But when the company rolled out its guarantee of on-time delivery, it found that customers felt that the faulty valves justified triggering the guarantee. The company could hardly argue; after all, if the gas wasn't accessible, it couldn't be considered an on-time delivery. Thus the company soon instituted a routine of checking every valve before shipping it out the door, virtually eliminating that source of guarantee triggerings.

Sometimes technology can help. The First National Bank of Chicago was continually criticized by customers for waiting too long before opening new windows when long lines formed. The problem was that the lines sometimes formed quickly, before busy tellers or managers could react. The bank finally came up with an unusual solution: It installed infrared heat sensors that could detect the presence of a large number of bodies. The moment lines started to build up, managers were alerted by the system and were able to bring more staff in before customers became irritated.

In some cases, a company has to take more extensive steps to address problems that come to light when a guarantee is rolled out. Quimobasicos found that it had difficulties getting chemicals from its factory in Monterrey to certain distributors in time to meet its guarantee of sufficient inventory. The company realized that the sheer distance between its factory and these distributors, many of which were located close to Mexico City, was part of the problem; even when the company knew that a distant distributor had suddenly run low on product, it wasn't always easy to get a truck to make the delivery run before the distributor ran out. So Quimobasicos opened a warehouse near Mexico City and started stockpiling product there, so that most distributors could be restocked within hours. It was a considerable investment, one that had never seemed necessary before the guarantee. But the company felt that the impression it made on customers by being able to honor its extraordinary guarantee was more than worth the trouble.

Delta Dental Plan: Turning the Negatives Into Positives

Delta Dental Plan was extremely aggressive in employing guarantee-related complaint data to improve its quality in a number of areas. Customers didn't like being placed on hold when they called, for example, even though Delta's phone pickup speed was already the fastest in the insurance business, with 42 percent of all calls answered within ten seconds and 100 percent within twenty seconds. In addition, customers complained about being transferred on the phone from one Delta employee to another.

To fix the problems, Delta cross-trained its employees and started having managers pick up phone calls, so that more people were available to help with any surge in incoming calls.

And because employees were more broadly trained, they didn't have to transfer calls from patients to one department, calls from customer administrators to another, and calls from dentists to a third. The company even replaced its standard cubicle walls with lower-walled versions, so employees could ask questions of one another and pass around paperwork without having to place customers on hold. As a result of these changes, the average phone pickup time was halved, and most calls were handled by whoever answered the phone, without any need to transfer callers. Not only did Delta achieve the improvement without hiring additional customer service people (except for two bilingual employees added in response to a customer with non-English-speaking employees), but the company saved $20,000 a month in its 800-number phone bill owing to the increased speed at which calls were handled.

Delta also made changes to address problems highlighted by customers who had triggered the guarantee of smooth conversion from another dental plan. Some of these customers complained that their problems hadn't been attended to quickly enough; others found errors or delays in subscriber I.D. cards, reports, and bills. To remedy the situation, Delta changed its policy of making sales managers responsible for their new clients' smooth conversion; instead, *all* employees were to consider it their job to handle new customers' problems, so that these problems could be dealt with on the spot without any of them slipping through the cracks. To reduce the errors, Delta instituted a series of checks and verifications of addresses and other data both when information was entered into the computer and, again, before materials were mailed out. The triggerings in these areas were soon reduced to a trickle.

A problem that at first appeared intractable was that Delta's payments on some claims were delayed by the necessity of waiting for information from other insurers who provided overlapping coverage for subscribers (for example, subscribers covered both by their employer's plan and by their spouse's employer's plan). Delta had no means of speeding up the response from other insurance companies, none of which seemed to share Delta's sense of urgency. But then the company realized that the dentists submitting the patient bills often had the needed co-insurance information in their own files; since their own payments were held up by Delta's lack of this information, the dentists were typically only too happy to supply the data and help Delta bypass the delays.

The Dynamic Guarantee

By speeding up its claims processing, Delta was able to exceed its guarantee of turning around 85 percent of all claims (during the policy year) within fifteen calendar days. Even more impressive, the company was able to turn around 99.5 percent of all claims within thirty days. But that accomplishment raised two questions. First, could the company now hope to raise its turnaround rate to 100 percent within thirty days? And second, should Delta *guarantee* such a rate?

Although Delta had been successful in raising its turnaround rate to the point where it was within a hair of 100 percent, the company knew that achieving that last 0.5 percent would be extraordinarily difficult and perhaps even impossible. There were just too many ways for a claim to be delayed. Even if the company could identify all sources of delay, eliminating each one of them would be extremely costly and time-consuming. And it wasn't as if the 99.5 percent rate was a significant source of dissatisfaction.

On the other hand, Delta knew from consulting with customers that the addition of a 100-percent-within-thirty-days statement to its guarantee would be extremely impressive. One hundred percent is the ultimate milestone; it suggests strength and confidence, whereas 85 percent or even 99.5 percent, as impressive as these achievements may be, actually serve to call attention to where the company is falling short.

The question thus boiled down to the following: Should Delta strengthen its guarantee with a promise of 100 percent turnaround within thirty days *even though it knew it couldn't quite meet that goal*? Assuming that the company had to pay out every time it exceeded the thirty-day limit, the 100 percent guarantee would cost $30,000 a year. That's not an insignificant sum, but it might be far outweighed by the extra business generated for the company by the stronger guarantee. Besides, the higher guarantee would serve to inspire the company to strive to narrow the 0.5 percent gap. But then again, mightn't some customers be irritated to find that the company couldn't quite live up to its guarantee?

Delta is still mulling over the question. But the situation points to an important aspect of guarantees that many companies overlook: A guarantee should be regarded not as a static fixture but as a dynamic, evolving entity. This is not to say that a company should revamp its guarantee every six months; indeed a company like L. L. Bean would be crazy to tinker with its celebrated guarantee. But most companies will profit from at least considering the ways in which its guarantee might be fine-tuned, whether to address shortcomings in the original guarantee or to take advantage of new opportunities raised by changes in the marketplace or the company itself.

Domino's: Upping the Ante

Domino's was one company that decided it needed to tinker with its guarantee. The problem: Customer surveys revealed that its celebrated thirty-minute-delivery-or-it's-free guarantee was considered too generous—so generous, in fact, that many customers whose pizza was a little late felt guilty about accepting a free pizza. As a result, the guarantee was often left untriggered by customers receiving late pizzas, which meant both that customers weren't being compensated and that the company wasn't getting an accurate picture of how well it was living up to its promise.

The fix was simple: Domino's reduced the payout on its on-time guarantee from a free pizza to three dollars off. Whatever money the company might have saved by paying less per triggering was overwhelmed by the jump in the number of triggerings—which was just what the company wanted. These extra triggerings didn't represent an increase in late deliveries; it was just that now the late deliveries were coming to light, and customers had something to show for it. To make extra sure that triggerings were reflecting the number of late deliveries, the president of the Baltimore-area Domino's outlets, which strictly enforce the guarantee, would show up unannounced at his restaurants and ask delivery people what they would do if they were a few minutes late and the customer didn't say anything about it. Those deliverers who said that they would take off the three dollars anyway received a $50 cash bonus on the spot. Unlike other Domino's nationwide, the Baltimore Domino's even kept the guarantee in force during snowstorms, knowing full well that thirty-minute delivery was impossible in those conditions.

More recently, Domino's has tried out an even bolder guarantee: total satisfaction. Under this program, the company would allow customers to call up the restaurant, tell whoever answered that they simply didn't like the pizza, and get a free one quickly delivered to their door. The company may even be considering instituting this satisfaction guarantee in place of the thirty-minute guarantee. After all, Domino's speedy delivery capabilities are already well-established; indeed, much of the public perceives that Domino's drivers pose a risk on the roads because of their obsession with delivering pizzas on time (although this perception appears to be something of an urban myth). Domino's suspects that it could now make greater inroads in market share by employing a guarantee that addressed the issue of the quality of its pizza. In fact, soon after testing out the new guarantee, Domino's changed the recipe for its pizza, thickening the crust and adding more cheese and toppings—a good example of the interrelationship between quality and a powerful guarantee.

Oakley Millwork is also planning to modify its guarantee. Right now, it promises customers that whatever they order will be in stock by the promised delivery date. It has been an extremely effective guarantee, but Oakley wants to go further; it is now considering guaranteeing that the order will contain no errors. If the customer claims that a delivered item is the wrong one, the customer will get the right item free—even if Oakley can prove that it was the customer's error and not its own. The mistake may be the customer's, but Oakley believes that it's not a matter of fault but of customer dissatisfaction; if the customer doesn't like what he's received from Oakley, he shouldn't have to pay for it.

Guarantees can even be revamped on a crisis basis. Sears had always offered a standard warranty on repair work performed at its auto shops. But when the state of California in 1992 accused the company of frequently performing shoddy and unnecessary work, the company quickly turbocharged its guarantee: Any customer who felt that he or she had been poorly treated by Sears' auto shops could show up at the shop and get a refund on the spot, with no proof of shoddy or bogus work required. Furthermore, to ensure that the repair scandal didn't hurt sales of its relatively high-quality Diehard battery and Roadhandler tire lines, Sears was soon heavily advertising beefed-up versions of the already strong guarantees on these products. The Diehard battery guarantee was expanded to include free roadside service for customers whose batteries died, and the Roadhandler guarantee was expanded to cover tire damage resulting from road hazards—nails, rocks, curbs, and the like—which are normally excluded from tire guarantees. In addition, an unconditional guarantee of satisfaction was tacked on to both products. All these guarantee changes went a long way toward containing the damage done by the repair allegations.

Changing the guarantee program doesn't necessarily require changing the guarantee itself. Quimobasicos plans to increase the impact of its guarantee simply by offering it to a wider range of distributors and for a wider range of products. In addition, the company is going to roll out a "pass-through" version of the guarantee, so that the end-users of its chemicals—that is, the customers of its distributors—will be guaranteed that the distributor will have the product they want in stock; if not, Quimobasicos will compensate them as well as the distributor.

Marriott: Making Sure Guest Complaints Are Addressed

A company may want to tinker not with the guarantee itself but with the guarantee-triggering and complaint-gathering mechanisms. Marriott had set up a complaint hotline that guests were encouraged to use in case of any problems; the call was then routed to the department responsible for the problem—to engineering, for example, if the air conditioning was broken, or to housekeeping if more towels were needed. But the company was dismayed to learn that too many of these complaints were never followed up after they were received. The problem was that no one at the hotel was taking responsibility for making sure that the complaints were addressed.

To cope with the situation, Marriott is trying a multipronged approach to gathering complaint feedback. First, a rapid response card labeled "Need help? Have an idea?" is placed in each room. The card lists two in-house, two-digit phone numbers. The first allows guests to leave a recorded message, and is intended to solicit complaints from customers who find it awkward to directly confront a staff person. The second reaches a guest relations manager, who represents the hotel's general manager; the guest relations manager is on site twenty-four hours a day and has the responsibility for handling all complaints and problems in a guaranteed response time of thirty minutes. The rapid response card also encourages departing guests to write down on the spaces provided any complaints, suggestions, or comments about the hotel staff or accommodations. The paper jacket that contains the guest's check-in receipt also asks for written comments. With all these avenues available to guests to register their feelings, Marriott hopes that few dissatisfied-but-silent customers will be leaving its hotels.

Is It Worth It?

While it is often clear to managers that the implementation of an extraordinary guarantee has had a strong, positive effect on quality, customer loyalty, and profits, quantifying the guarantee's contribution to these benefits can be difficult. Nevertheless, some companies have made an effort to do so. The results are impressive.

Take, for example, the eighteen Domino's outlets in the Baltimore area that enforce the guarantee more strictly than

most other Domino's. These eighteen restaurants have a nonre-
turning customer rate of 1.8 percent—the lowest among the
3,800 Domino's in the United States. When the Marriott Hotel
chain started guaranteeing its room service, sales increased
immediately and surveys revealed that the percentage of customers satisfied with various aspects of the service jumped
between five and ten percentage points in every category.

JWS's late delivery rate dropped from 5 percent before the
guarantee to less than 0.5 percent after the guarantee. The
company pays out about $35,000 a year on the guarantee, plus
another $35,000 in employee bonuses for error-free days. But
that $70,000 cost is dwarfed by the fact that sales have risen 7
percent in a depressed market; in addition, its guarantee-
driven efforts to become more efficient have cut a number of
operating costs, including two-thirds of its overtime hours.
First Image brought in $600,000 in new business attributed by
customers to the guarantee in one four-month period alone,
and cut the costs of its microfilm processing operations; meanwhile, guarantee payouts have been a mere 0.14 percent of
revenues.

Delta Dental Plan has been exceptionally thorough in
surveying customers to determine the effect of its extraordinary
guarantee. As a result, the company knows that the guarantee
was primarily responsible for raising its customer retention rate
from 97 percent to 99 percent, a 2 percent jump worth $19
million a year. In addition, the guarantee has been responsible
for half its growth in new subscribers. Meanwhile, administrative costs for its insurance programs have dropped nearly 11
percent—at a time when health insurance administrative costs
have on average been rising rapidly. Guarantee payouts were
budgeted at $90,000 the first year of the program, but have
turned out to be only $15,000.

Hampton Inn also meticulously tracked the costs and
benefits of its guarantee of satisfaction. The company found
that in 1990, the first year of the guarantee program, about 2
percent of its guests, representing 157,000 room-nights, were
persuaded to stay at the hotel because of the guarantee, bringing in an additional $7 million. More than 3,300 guests who
had invoked the guarantee returned to a Hampton Inn that

same year, and 61 percent of these people said that they returned specifically because of the guarantee; retaining these guests brought in an extra $1 million that year. In addition, nearly half the guests who didn't invoke the guarantee said that they were more likely to stay again at a Hampton Inn because of the guarantee. Not even counting this last group, the guarantee thus contributed an extra $8 million to revenues in 1990—a year in which the company paid out a mere $350,000 in payouts. The next year's results were even more dramatic: The company estimated that the incremental revenue attributable to the guarantee jumped to $18 million, whereas the level of payouts remained flat.

The results from these companies suggest that extraordinary guarantees can give the corporate bottom line a significant lift. Of course, such cost/benefit calculations don't even take into consideration less tangible benefits, such as improved employee morale (85 percent of Hampton Inn employees, for example, said that the guarantee motivates them to do a better job), better management decision making, and improved quality processes. These "softer" benefits should prove to be as important as company profitability.

It may be an overstatement to say that an extraordinary guarantee can single-handedly transform an organization from a basket case to a powerhouse. But clearly a guarantee can act as a catalyst for, and lay the foundation for, a much-needed revitalization.

Chapter 10

Legal and Ethical Issues

Many companies that have implemented extraordinary guarantees report that their legal departments were dead set against the guarantees. There are generally three reasons for the objections: (1) There are few formal legal guidelines regarding the establishment of extraordinary guarantees; (2) the terms of the guarantee are not legally precise; and (3) the guarantees entail unpredictable levels of risk.

The lack of legal guidelines does not reflect an absence of guarantee or warranty law. As discussed in Chapter 2, the Magnuson-Moss Warranty Act of 1974 and the various state laws based on the Uniform Commercial Code establish ample direction as to the legal requirements of guarantees and warranties. But these laws and regulations are for the most part addressed to the *minimum* protection that a company must offer. Businesses offering guarantees that go well above and beyond are largely on their own in terms of predicting how courts might interpret any ambiguity in their written promises. If a resort guarantees that "it will do whatever it takes to make you happy," it's not entirely clear what would happen if a customer sued the resort for several thousand dollars on the grounds that it refused to pay to fly in the customer's friends, which is what would have made her happy.

Obviously, being clear about what is being promised and what will be paid out if the promise isn't kept is the key to avoiding such legal debacles. But one of the most important tenets of extraordinary guarantees is that they must be as simple, strong, and unconditional as possible. A guarantee *is* a legal contract, but it shouldn't *read* like a legal contract; it should read like a personal promise. Thus there will always be loopholes that a creatively unscrupulous customer could take advantage of. As we shall see in the next chapter, conniving customers generally do not turn out to be much of a threat as a practical matter. But legal departments are paid to close loopholes, and will probably not be comfortable with an extraordinary guarantee unencumbered by protective clauses. One can imagine how L. L. Bean's guarantee would read if a legal department had a free hand to modify it: "If for any reason, except as noted in clauses 1a, 1b, and 1c below, you are not satisfied, where "satisfied" is defined as. . . ."

Extraordinary guarantees pose certain risks whose magnitudes are difficult to calculate. Lawyers, being in general risk-averse, may focus on these risks. One risk is that a large number of customers will trigger the guarantee, causing significant financial damage. There is little protection against this risk other than the company's confidence in its own products or services; indeed, it is the assumption of this confidence that makes a powerful guarantee appealing to customers.

Another risk is that an extraordinary guarantee could conceivably increase a company's exposure to consequential liability—that is, the responsibility for damage or injury caused by the product or service. There is no strong legal precedent for holding a company especially liable for such damages simply because it offered a strong guarantee of quality or customer satisfaction. But it's not hard to picture a jury hammering a company that knowingly stuck a strong guarantee on a shoddy product or service that ultimately caused harm. After all, part of the point of a powerful guarantee is to inspire confidence in the producer's reliability and competence. A thirty-year guarantee might embolden the purchaser of a ladder to climb higher on it than he otherwise might; an unconditional guarantee of satisfaction might give the customer of an adventure travel service the confidence to try a hot-air balloon ride. If the ladder proved flimsy, or the balloon pilot inexperienced, and injury resulted, the guarantee could be seen as having contributed to the accident.

One solution is for companies not to stick extraordinary guarantees on subpar products or services, particularly those that entail risk to persons or property. Another is to provide clear statements of limited liability in, or with, the guarantee. Federal Express (which often ships valuables), AT&T (on whose services many companies' ability to operate is dependent), and a number of other high-quality manufacturers and service providers attach such statements to their extraordinary guarantees.

The drawback to these disclaimers, of course, is that they take away some of the impact of the guarantee. In addition, such statements do not always provide the desired protection against liability; courts often rule that stated liability limits are irrelevant if customers have been misled into thinking such limits don't apply. The U.S. Postal Service, for example, was ordered by the courts to reimburse a customer for the loss of a $7,500 watch shipped by insured mail, even though the customer had signed a standard agreement that limited the service's responsibility for valuables to $500. The customer claimed that a postal clerk had told him otherwise, however, and the courts found the customer's claim more compelling than the Postal Service's fine print.

Could a company suddenly back out of an exceptional guarantee if it proved problematic? It would certainly have difficulty refusing to honor the guarantee for those customers who purchased the product or service while the guarantee was in effect (with the possible exception of customers who intended to abuse the guarantee, a situation I will discuss in the next chapter)—unless the company specifically stated on its guarantee that it could be revoked without notice, a statement that would surely weaken the guarantee in many customers' eyes.

Disarming the guarantee for new customers, however, should simply require ceasing to present the guarantee—that is, removing it from packaging, written materials, and promotional displays. A thorny problem could arise, however, if the guarantee had been heavily advertised. In that case, new customers might claim that the guarantee had been drilled into their heads, and that the disappearance of such advertising did not necessarily signal that the guarantee wasn't in force. The company could, of course, clearly promote the fact that a weaker guarantee is in effect, but a more reasonable course of action would probably be to budget for a dwindling stream of payouts after the guarantee has been revoked. In any event, the negative marketing consequences of removing a powerful guarantee will probably be a far greater problem than having to pay out on it after it has been revoked; the best bet is to approach such guarantees more carefully in the first place.

While senior executives will of course want to consult their legal counsel when designing and implementing an extraordinary guarantee, they will also have to be prepared to override many of the lawyers' objections. It is the lawyers' job to envision and protect against worst-case scenarios; it is management's job to take a more balanced view and to embrace risk when the potential payoff is high enough. As an interesting example of how overly cautious lawyers can be with regard to guarantees, one California law firm aired radio commercials in which it allotted precious seconds at the end to note that it couldn't guarantee results. Only a law firm would so prominently stick an "antiwarranty" on its advertising campaign. As Marc Grainer, chairman of management consultancy TARP Institute, was quoted in *Forbes* as saying on the subject of guarantees: "Get the attorneys involved early, but then shoot them."[1]

The Ethics of Guarantees

In general, offering an extraordinary guarantee is anything but unethical. Indeed, it is easier to make the case that a company that refuses to stand behind its products or services with a powerful guarantee is not operating ethically. There are, however, possible exceptions. One is offering a powerful guarantee with a shoddy product or service. If the guarantee is offered with the full intention of honoring the guarantee while improving quality, then it may be more a question of bad timing and judgment than of unethical behavior. But there can be no benefit of the doubt for a company that strongly guarantees an inferior product or service in the hope that most customers won't bother to invoke the guarantee, or—even worse—if the company has no intention of paying out on the guarantee, planning instead either to tie customers up in red tape or to disappear in the night with the profits.

Thornier questions of ethics arise respecting the use of extraordinary guarantees by some professional service firms, where higher-than-normal ethical standards may apply because of the complex nature of these services. The United States Supreme Court, for example, in ruling on prohibitions on advertising in the legal profession, said that "because the public lacks sophistication concerning legal services, misstatements that might be overlooked or deemed unimportant in other advertising may be found quite inappropriate in legal advertising."[2]

In general, codes of ethics and professional conduct in regard to marketing communications adhere to the guidelines established by the Federal Trade Commission regarding false, fraudulent, and misleading advertising. Certain types of marketing communications have been flagged as having significant potential for deception. The American Medical Association, for example, in its *1992 Current Opinions on Ethical and Judicial Affairs*, says that a statement which implies that a physician has cured or successfully treated a large number of cases involving a particularly serious ailment is deceptive if it implies a certainty of result and creates unjustified and misleading expectations in prospective patients.[3]

Might guarantees also be considered inappropriate? Indeed, the Association of Management Consulting Firms (ACME) hints in its ethical guidelines that this may be the case, stating: "We will present our qualifications for serving a client solely in terms of our competence, experience, and standing, and we will not guarantee any specific result, such as amount of cost reduction or profit increase." Although this statement may not apply to unconditional guarantees, it suggests that guarantees in general may be suspect.

The main ethical concern about guarantees centers on the question of misleading potential clients. A guarantee would be considered unethical if it suggested that the provider has a greater degree of competence than he or she actually has or if the guarantee erroneously implies a certainty of result. A physician, for example, wouldn't guarantee the results of a nonroutine surgical procedure or the outcome of treatment of a serious disease. Even the offer of a complete refund would not mitigate the injustice of claiming certainty of result, since such a payout would not cover all of the client's costs, such as the lost time and aggravation (or worse) caused by the service failure.

Guarantees can be offered even in the medical community, however, if there is reasonable certainty that the stated results will occur. Mission Oaks Hospital in Los Gatos, California, for example, guarantees that if a patient has to wait longer than five minutes for emergency-room care, the bill will be reduced by 25 percent. The vast majority of the hospital's emergency-care patients do, in fact, receive care within that specified time. For the same reason, unconditional guarantees in the legal profession would probably first turn up without much controversy for such services as uncontested divorce, uncontested name change, uncontested adoption, the preparation of simple wills and tax returns, probate services, and certain real estate matters.

There is also the issue of various professions' "dignity standard," which exists to discourage marketing communications that seek to influence consumers through emotional factors not relevant to professional competence. In the legal profession, for example, there is pressure to refrain from "overt self-promotion," in the interests of the public and as a sign of personal integrity and professional independence. ACME cautions its members against advertising their services in "self-laudatory language or in any other manner derogatory to the dignity of the profession." Although part of the motivation in prohibiting "undignified" marketing practices is a desire to avoid tarnishing a profession's polished image, there is also a genuine danger that a guarantee not presented in a dignified manner might mislead the public in some way. For example, in appealing to fears of loss, guarantees may distract clients away from evaluating a firm's quality toward evaluating the service primarily in terms of risk exposure.

Another problem arises for professional service firms that offer a guarantee for which the payout takes the form of a performance contract ("no money due until . . ."). Such a guarantee is basically a contingent fee—that is, a fee received for services performed on behalf of a client, payable to the provider if, and only if, some result is achieved through the provider's efforts. If the client does not obtain the desired results, the provider is not entitled to payment. The chief argument in favor of a contingent fee, from the standpoint of the firm, is that it gives the firm the financial incentive to use its best efforts to maximize its clients' satisfaction or meet targeted goals. From the standpoint of the client, the contingency fee functions as a hedge. The client's exposure to loss is limited by the amount of the payout.

The major arguments against the contingent fee are that it puts pressure on the provider that is inconsistent with the detachment essential to the practice of the profession; that it creates conflicts of interest; and that it affects professionals' judgment as to the nature and extent of the services they should offer. ACME advises its members to assume an independent position with clients, making certain that their advice is based on impartial consideration of all pertinent facts and responsible opinions. Further, notes ACME, its members should "not serve a client under terms or conditions that might impair (their) objectivity, independence, or integrity." It would be naive to assume that the threat of nonpayment, as implied in a refund or performance contract, cannot influence a professional's judgment. The problem is whether the influence will cause the provider to serve the client better or encourage the provider to take shortcuts.

Given the increasingly competitive business climate in which professional service firms must operate, it is only natural that traditional standards that seek to curtail marketing efforts on ethical grounds have loosened somewhat. The legal profession has been a microcosm and model for that change. In 1977, the U.S. Supreme Court held that blanket prohibitions against lawyer advertising were unconstitutional infringements of the First Amendment. Subsequent Supreme Court decisions have since whittled away most restrictions on advertising except those that prohibit false and misleading advertising.

It is likely that any marketing techniques that encourage

client confidence without being materially misleading will eventually be accepted to some extent by most professional service communities. By forcing firms to stand behind their work, guarantees may even be seen ultimately as increasing the stature of a profession.

Notes

1. "How'm I Doin?" *Forbes* (December 24, 1990): 106.
2. Bates et al. v. State Bar of Arizona, 433 S.S. 350 (97 S. Ct. 2691 1977).
3. Opinion 5.02, *1992 Current Opinions on Ethical and Judicial Affairs* (Chicago: American Medical Association, 1992).

Chapter 11

Cheating

When first considering the merits of an extraordinary guarantee program, many managers come to an abrupt halt on one issue: cheating. Is there anything, they wonder, to prevent a customer who obtains a high-quality product or service from lying, claiming dissatisfaction with it and the right to a payout? For these managers, customer cheating represents the Achilles' heel of an extraordinary guarantee, exposing the company to enormous risk.

Although the concern is a rational one, and perfectly natural, the fact is that customer cheating almost never turns out to be a significant problem among companies offering extraordinary guarantees. The fear of cheating must be kept in perspective, and should not be allowed to poison a company's efforts to build quality and satisfy customers through a powerful guarantee. Instead of expending large amounts of time and resources installing guarantee-weakening provisions to thwart that one percent or less of customers who would stoop to cheating, managers would be better off concentrating their attention on better serving the vast majority of customers who are honest. Nonetheless, the potential for cheating can't be totally ignored.

The Extent of Cheating

Customer cheating on a guarantee can take any of several forms, including:

- Falsely claiming to have experienced those conditions required to trigger a guarantee (dissatisfaction, for example, or poor product performance)
- Purposely causing those conditions to occur (by abusing a product, or making it impossible for a service to be delivered as promised)
- Entering into a purchase with the intent of triggering the guarantee, regardless of the quality of the product or service (for example, buying a product, then later returning it under the guarantee so as to have had free use of it for a time)

A few businesses really do seem to have a problem with cheating. According to an article in *The Wall Street Journal* (June 3, 1992), some upscale clothing stores with no-questions-asked return policies are plagued with shoppers who buy expensive clothes to wear to parties and then return them a few days later. Department stores that don't require receipts for returns often suspect that they are taking back goods from other stores. In an extreme example, one store in the chain of Burdine's department stores in Florida discovered that a significant percentage of its receiptless returns were for items that had been shoplifted from the store.

Fortunately, the great majority of businesses that have made an effort to pin down the extent of guarantee cheating have decided that the problem is a minor one. Even among retailers, believed to have the highest incidence of cheating, surveys suggest that cheating runs between 2 and 5 percent of all returns. When taking into account the fact that the cost of handling a return is generally only a fraction of the cost of the item, the total cost of cheating to a retailer is typically far less than one percent of revenues.

Why People Cheat

There are three main reasons why people cheat on extraordinary guarantees: They want to test the system, they want revenge, or they're after material gain.

One form of testing the system is "hacking": a pranklike act undertaken for the pleasure of defeating a form of protection, in this case the conditions of a specific guarantee. Thus some Domino's outlets found that a number of college students were stationing themselves in hard-to-locate addresses when ordering pizzas so as to be sure to collect on the thirty-minute delivery guarantee. Another, more benign form of testing the system is triggering a guarantee just to see if the company will honor it. This form of cheating occurs when a guarantee seems so generous and so easy to invoke that a customer simply can't resist seeing if it's for real.

Revenge is likely to be a motive for cheating on a guarantee if a company has a history of providing poor service or product quality, or if the company has done something to offend a customer. Customers may cheat to get revenge for prior bad service experiences for which they feel they were not fairly compensated, or they may cheat in order to stockpile "credits" for expected future service failures. Frequent fliers routinely subjected to service ineptitude by a particular airline would be prime candidates for cheating on a guarantee offered by that airline. For this reason, companies with poor quality records need to pay off their bad-quality debts to customers by revamping their quality processes and reestablishing credibility before offering a powerful guarantee.

Customers may also cheat because they don't like the company or something the company represents, even if the company hasn't done anything offensive to them personally. Exxon and Continental, for example, have racked up so much bad publicity for their perceived affronts to the environment and labor, respectively, that these two companies could expect higher-than-average rates of cheating were they to offer any sort of extraordinary guarantee. In effect, customers would be invoking the guarantee as a form of protest, regardless of the quality of the service or product. Revenge cheating may also be inspired by a price hike—especially a price hike accompanying the introduction of a guarantee. Even if the service improves as a result of the guarantee, customers may feel justified in falsely invoking it just to get their money's worth.

There are customers, of course, who cheat just for material

gain. The idea of getting something for nothing appeals to most of us, and some of us can't resist the temptation when it is dangled in front of our faces. Especially for people unburdened by consciences, the incentive to cheat for material gain increases with the size of the payout. Ironically, for people with only a little larceny in their blood the reverse is probably true: They would probably feel guilty taking a large payout under false pretenses, but might succumb to the temptation of claiming, say, a free hamburger.

Certain factors may make it easier emotionally for customers to cheat. Many people would be more inclined to cheat a large company than a small company, for example, especially if the large company is not a local employer. The rationale here is that a large company is better able to absorb the costs, and is perceived as more impersonal and unfeeling. Customers may also find it easier to lie if their claims are handled by cold, indifferent personnel. And cheating is also less emotionally wrenching if it is inflicted on a company with which they are unlikely to do business again, such as an out-of-town restaurant.

Dealing With Cheaters

A number of strategies can be employed to cut down on cheating. These include moving to specific guarantees, adding conditions, refusing to pay, revoking a guarantee, targeting different customers, and personalizing the complaint process.

Instead of offering unconditional guarantees, which rely on customer perception as the final criterion of product or service excellence, companies can cut down on some types of cheating by offering specific guarantees that employ objectively measurable performance standards. Asserting dissatisfaction is easy, but falsely claiming that a meal arrived late or that an appliance doesn't work requires more involved acts of deception, and many potential cheaters won't bother. Unfortunately, as discussed earlier, specific guarantees often lack the impact of unconditional guarantees. In most cases, a company will lose more in marketing and quality improvement benefits by downgrading its guarantee than it will gain from reducing cheating.

Besides, it isn't always the case that a more specific, harder-to-cheat-on guarantee will do better at fending off would-be cheaters—especially if hackers are a problem. The students cheating Domino's were largely motivated by the fact that ingenuity was required to trigger the pizza chain's speedy-delivery guarantee. In such cases, quite the opposite tack may work, as the Massachusetts Institute of Technology discovered when dealing with its computer hackers. MIT students in the 1960s and 1970s were world-famous for their ability to get into the innards of the school's software and "crash," or temporarily disable, the entire system. The more sophisticated the security, the more ingenious the hackers became. Finally, MIT tried a new approach: It removed all security, making it a snap for any student to crash the system. The hacking came to a screeching halt; with the challenge removed, crashing the system became not a brilliant feat to be admired but a mindless act of vandalism.

In the same way, companies plagued by guarantee hackers may want to consider the possibility that, contrary to what their intuition tells them, the easier it is to trigger the guarantee, the less likely it is that customers will want to cheat. If a company offers an unconditional guarantee of satisfaction, for example, then the mechanism for cheating is trivial: One need only say that one is dissatisfied. Most students are not inherently dishonest; they just like a good challenge to go with their free pizza.

Cheating can also be reduced by making it harder for the customer to prove that the conditions of the guarantee triggering have been met. Airline guarantees, for example, have typically required several forms of documentation proving that the customer did indeed take the flight in question and that a guarantee-covered problem actually occurred. But while such barriers undoubtedly cut down on impulse cheating, they also inflict unnecessary difficulties on honest customers with legitimate complaints. Making it difficult for customers to invoke a guarantee compounds their aggravation and reduces the company's chance of regaining their loyalty and of identifying sources of error.

A company can, of course, simply refuse to pay someone suspected of cheating. In the case of a specific guarantee, a company can take pains to track the conditions governing the triggering of the guarantee; if by its own reckoning the conditions aren't met, it can deny the claim of a customer who insists they are. But along the way, the company will end up deeply offending many honest customers who mistakenly believe that the conditions have been met—who feel, for example, that the service was much too slow, even if it was actually delivered within the promised time frame.

Even companies offering unconditional guarantees can identify and turn away cheaters. Many companies, for example, set up computer data bases to keep track of customers who invoke the guarantee; if a name turns up too often, the customer can be denied the payout. Theoretically, such a customer could sue the company, claiming that the guarantee doesn't say anything about frequent invokers. In the unlikely case that this occurred, and in the equally unlikely case that the company wished to fight back forcefully through the courts, the company could bring an action against the customer based on those laws, found in most states, which protect companies against the intent to commit fraud. After all, a customer would have a tough time convincing a judge that he or she was truly dissatisfied with a service or product that he or she repeatedly purchased.

A kinder and gentler approach to dealing with frequent invokers is to send them a letter apologizing for not being able to satisfy them and inviting them to do business elsewhere. Several retailers do this; so does Hampton Inn. (One Hampton Inn guest who had repeatedly invoked the no-pay guarantee night after night actually wrote on a comment card that he liked Hampton Inns because they were "free.") Most customers so notified immediately take the hint; the company can only hope that it hasn't turned away too many honest customers.

In order to cut down on the number of people who make a habit of buying items at other stores and then returning them at Wal-Mart, the chain tracks receiptless returners, asks frequent returners to present a receipt, and if they can't or won't, eventually stops accommodating them. The Burdine's store in Florida that was suffering through the return of shoplifted items, on the other hand, had to take more drastic action: The store completely revoked its policy of accepting no-receipt returns. The problem with revoking a generous guarantee policy in this way is that it affects honest along with dishonest customers, and deprives the company of the operational, marketing, and strategic benefits to be gained from an extraordinary guarantee. Clearly, revocation should be a last resort.

Another approach to cutting down on cheating is to personalize the complaint process. People will be much less inclined to lie if they must face a friendly, courteous customer service person to register a claim. When customers perceive organizations as collections of human beings like themselves, instead of as faceless bureaucracies with bulging pockets, they will be more likely to think twice about defrauding them. And needless to say, providing personal, friendly service offers many other rewards besides reducing cheating.

There will always be cheaters. To deal with them, companies can raise barriers and limit their generosity, but in doing so they will also reduce their ability to provide exceptional service to honest customers. At the very least, obsessing about cheaters invariably results in undercutting the power of an extraordinary guarantee program.

In the end, it comes down to trust. As one executive tells his staff, if you don't trust your customers, you're in the wrong business. Or as another manager puts it, treat customers right, and the last thing they'll think about is finding ways to cheat you.

Index